IN A MONASTERY GARDEN

IN A MONASTERY GARDEN

Elizabeth & Reginald Peplow

DAVID & CHARLES

Newton Abbot · London · North Pomfret (Vt)

ACKNOWLEDGEMENTS

We thank the many monks, nuns, canons and gardeners who helped us with our research when visiting monasteries and cathedrals. We are also very grateful to Jill Davies for her secretarial help.

Photographs were provided courtesy of: page 9 Walter Scott; page 41 Janet & Colin Bord; page 56 The National Museum of Wales; page 131 The Sunday Times (artist Kate Osborne); page 139 National Motor Museum, Beaulieu; page 149 Beric Tempest Co Ltd.

The photographs on the following pages were provided by R Peplow: 39, 42, 46, 51, 85, 136, 143, 147, 150, 154, 155, 161.

British Library Cataloguing in Publication Data

Peplow, Elizabeth
  In a monastery garden.
  1. Great Britain. Religious buildings.
  Gardens to 1988
  I. Title II. Peplow, Reginald
  712′.7

  ISBN 0-7153-8966-1

Design by John Youé & Associates Ltd
Illustrations by Ron Tiner pages: 7, 13, 15, 17, 19, 21, 25, 27, 29, 31, 37, 43, 45, 53, 54, 57, 61, 65, 69, 71, 75, 89, 92, 93, 95, 97, 98, 99, 104, 107, 111, 117, 119, 122, 123, 127, 133, 134. Susan Claypole White pages: 34, 35, 50, 62, 78, 79, 110, 113, 114, 115, 124, 125, 130. Joyce Tuhill pages: 3, 48, 49, 83, 86, 87, 94, 96, 108, 129, 166.
Typeset by Typesetters (Birmingham) Ltd
Smethwick, West Midlands
and printed in Italy
by New Interlitho S.p.A., Milan
for David & Charles Publishers plc
Brunel House   Newton Abbot   Devon

Published in the United States of America
by David & Charles Inc
North Pomfret   Vermont 05053   USA

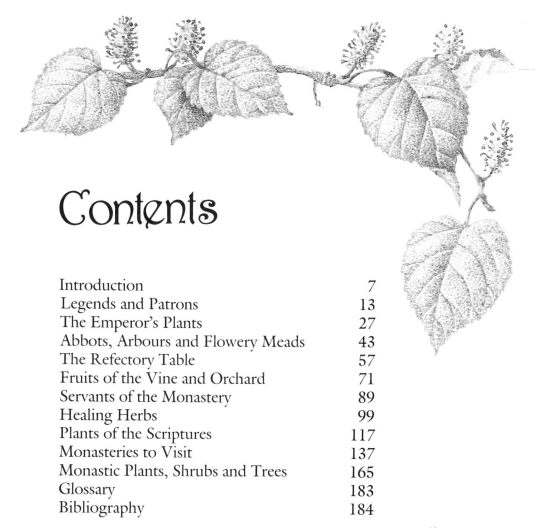

Contents

Introduction	7
Legends and Patrons	13
The Emperor's Plants	27
Abbots, Arbours and Flowery Meads	43
The Refectory Table	57
Fruits of the Vine and Orchard	71
Servants of the Monastery	89
Healing Herbs	99
Plants of the Scriptures	117
Monasteries to Visit	137
Monastic Plants, Shrubs and Trees	165
Glossary	183
Bibliography	184

Introduction

If, on a warm afternoon in the summer of 1537, you had chanced to be at a certain country fair in the Cotswolds, you might have observed an authoritative but cheerful monk in a black habit talking briskly with a seller of agricultural sundries. You would have been struck, perhaps, by his eagerness to examine every item on display and to extract from the vendor every available morsel of information, news and advice. You may have smiled, as those about you would have done, when the vendor, weary of the barrage of questions, pushed a tiny pouch of seeds into the hands of his friendly but troublesome inquisitor and bade him take his enquiries elsewhere.

It would be wrong to say that the monk Stephen – for that was his name – had a passionate interest in horticulture and thought about little else. He had, during his twenty or so years at the monastery, done everything required of him and often, some said, a great deal more. But often, when roused from his sleep at one o'clock in the morning for the night office, his dreams had been of new types of peaches that grew fat and luscious on the wall and rarely fell early to the ground; and, in the summer evenings after compline, when, according to St Benedict's Rule, he and his fellows retired in silence to their cells, he had suffered grave difficulty in forgetting his wish to spend just one more hour in the garden.

Stephen had known little of the strange ways of soil and the mysteries of plant growth when, as a young man, he had caught the attention of the busy porter at the gate-house and sought entry to the monastic community.

Coming from a wealthy family with some influence in the area, he had expected the great door to open to him at once, but he was kept waiting with the beggars and the wandering tradesmen for several days, even at times being handed the leavings of a monk's dinner as his sustenance for the night. Finally, however, having demonstrated his ability to be patient, he was allowed to take his place among the novices on the strict understanding that if he failed in any respect he would be escorted back to the gate-house and set on the road for home.

Like most other members of the community, Stephen spent much of his time in the cloisters – the four covered walks with an inner garden or area of grass called the cloister garth. This quadrangle was usually a hive of activity and in his earlier years in the monastery this was the place where he had toiled at his studies of monastic observance under the novice master and practised the chants and melodies of the divine office. It was the place, too, where the older brethren sat at their wooden desks studying their devotional or learned books, writing and illustrating manuscripts or discussing questions related to ecclesiastical learning or regular observance.

In later years, particularly on the day when he was appointed to the important position of monk-gardener and took on the responsibility of growing produce for the whole community and their guests, Stephen looked back on his year as a novice with nostalgia, for it was then that he had first fallen in love with a garden. It was a fairly small plot which had been tended carefully by servants under the casual direction of a senior monk and was set a little way from the busy cloisters against the infirmary wall. Here, on one of those rare afternoons when he had been able to walk alone for an hour, he had chanced to find the garden as one of the servants was harvesting mint for strewing on the infirmary floor. The plant's aroma inspired Stephen as nothing had done before.

Once inside the garden, among the brightly coloured peonies, the subtle greenery of the marjoram and the strange, heady perfume of the rosemary, Stephen was reluctant to leave. He returned as often as he could and marvelled at the fast growth of the many plants and the

Lincoln Cathedral
The Cloister Court,
looking south-west

8

way in which cuttings taken by the servant grew so readily.

One day, taking leave from his studies by telling his master that he was unwell, Stephen hurried across the stable yard to the infirmary. As he ran his fingers through a clump of thyme, a voice enquired, 'What is your business here?' Stephen turned, expecting to find a fellow monk for whom he could invent an explanation, and the words dried on his lips. The abbot, father of the monastery and the one person he had learned to respect as representing Christ in the midst of the brethren, stood patiently awaiting an answer.

Stephen was punished with a beating and a diet of bread and water for a week, but both the abbot and the novice master were understanding men; although they were strict with the observances of St Benedict's rule, they had noted Stephen's mounting interest in the garden and knew that they could make use of this in the future.

Over the centuries, there had been many keen monk-gardeners like Stephen, for a garden or series of gardens was of prime importance to members of all but a few orders when they established new communities in remote areas of Great Britain. Stephen learned much about other monastery gardens when, as a result of increasing responsibilities, he began to travel the country on monastery business. The monks of his own community conversed rarely, except on occasions such as feast days, but at many other establishments guests such as Stephen could engage in conversation and would be listened to in guest-house, parlour, warming-house and even over meals. He took full advantage of these opportunities and consequently sought out fellow gardeners on every visit. He also carried with him a generous supply of roots, seeds and cuttings as gifts from his own community, while accepting with gratitude similar gifts from his hosts.

There were times when he would describe the healing qualities of herbs and how sore heads, insect bites, aching and broken limbs, pains in the stomach and all kinds of sickness could be cured or made less vicious by their use. At other times he would fall silent and listen intently as the monks from Gloucester spoke of new ways of grafting and caring for pears, plums, sweet cherries and apples; while those from Hereford told of the massive yields of their vineyards and the delights of mulberry, fig and quince; while a brother from Peterborough gave an account of a flourishing orchard that had been established by Abbot Godfrey more than two centuries earlier.

Stephen learned, too, of the special art of growing less exotic plants such as celery, cabbage, onions, leeks, shallots and lettuce so that they would be larger and tastier than the year before. And he became more acquainted with those whose entire life was centred around the stocking of fish-ponds, the making and storage of salt, the growing of timber for building and for fuel, and the cultivation of willows in osier beds for the making of strong baskets and containers.

But although Stephen was keen to acquire new stock and gardening information, his real hunger was for knowledge of the past. He frequently sat late at night listening to an elderly monk recounting the times when monasteries were sacked by marauding Danes or decimated by the plague. It was on such an occasion that Stephen first heard the name Walafrid Strabo, a ninth-century monk who wrote about the plants that grew in Europe and who was also a fine illustrator. 'Not unlike you, it seems,' remarked a kindly monk as he handed to Stephen a fine copy of one of Strabo's works. 'This is for you to borrow. Bring it back on your next visit.'

Stephen left early the next morning to return to his own monastery, loaded with such items as grafted red cherry bushes, a manuscript about apples, some melons, a few bulbs of a very fine lily he had seen decorating the altar on a previous visit, some cold rabbit for his supper and a bottle of the monk's own wine. He spent every free minute of the next month poring over the beautifully illustrated vellum sheets of Strabo's work which had lain for more than a century in one of the cloister cupboards. The prior, who was interested in the activities of the monk-gardener and did not wish to be outshone by the offerings of another establishment, asked Stephen if he had heard of a monastery in Switzerland where, it was understood, plans had been made to create a wonderful herb garden comprising sixteen raised beds, each with a named variety of herb.

'I have heard talk of nothing else,' replied Stephen, and the prior passed the young monk his greatest prize – the plans of the ninth-century herb garden at St Gall.

Four days later, Stephen's normally measured tread was quick and his essentially pale countenance was flushed as he filed with his fellow monks into the Chapter House and prepared to tell the community of his plans to make a large extension to the monastery gardens and to recruit scribes and illustrators to begin work on a major herbal for the benefit of monastic communities not just in Great Britain but throughout Europe.

The abbot, however, interrupted Stephen's enthusiastic lecture. 'Put away your plans, Brother Stephen,' he said, 'abandon your thoughts of a herbal. For in three days this holy place in which brothers have lived and worked and prayed for centuries will be no more. Our treasures will be taken to London or sold, the stones from our walls will be removed for the building of cattle sheds, the lead from our roof will be melted down and carried away.'

And it happened almost as the abbot had predicted, except that the desecration began within an hour of the ending of mass that day. With time only for his God and his garden, Stephen had not concerned himself with rumours of arguments between the abbot and the king's commissioners, who had been frequent visitors recently.

Together with his fellow monks, many elderly and infirm, Stephen was ejected from the place he had long known as home. Lying beneath a hedge that night, he contented himself with the thought that somewhere, some time soon, he would begin another garden.

The achievements of those who followed in his footsteps and perhaps shared his ambitions may be seen in the many beautiful monastery gardens in Great Britain. The gardens at Beaulieu Abbey, Peterborough, Michelham Priory, Bury St Edmunds, Worcester and Prinknash are fine examples. Indeed, many of the ruins which have no formal content of herbs, flowers, fruits or vines are gardens in themselves.

Legends and Patrons

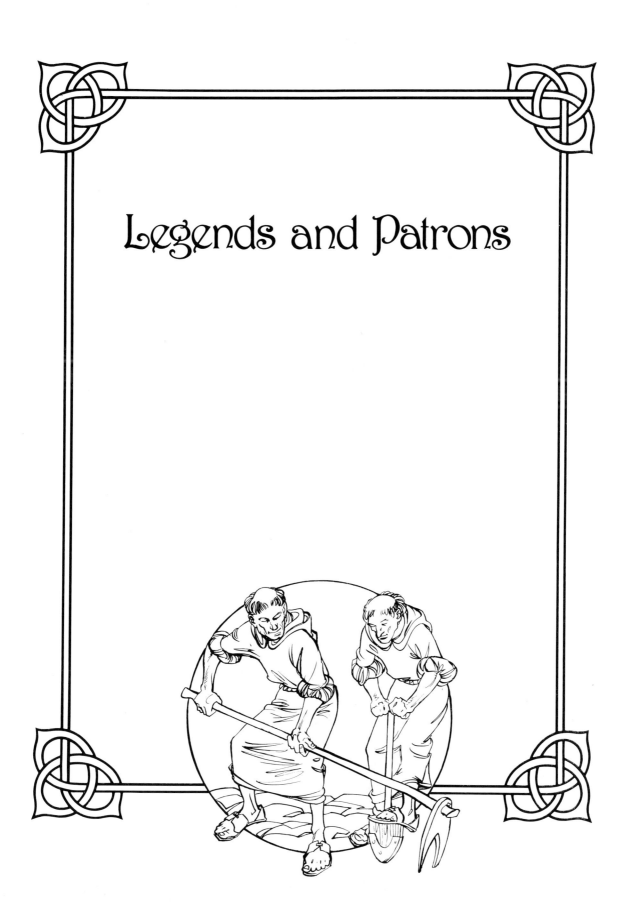

Any gardener who has pushed a piece of stick into the ground as a marker and found some weeks later that it has taken root and is producing leaf buds will understand how people with religious convictions took to their hearts the legend of the Glastonbury thorn tree.

According to legend, Philip, one of the twelve apostles, sent Joseph of Arimathea with Joseph, his son, and eleven more of his disciples to Britain and that they 'with great zeal and undaunted courage, preached the true and lively faith of Christ'. King Arviragus gave them 'a certain island in the west part of his dominions for their habitation, called Avalon, containing twelve hides of land, where they built a church of wreathen wands, and set a place apart for the burial of their servants'.

When offered the land, Joseph pushed his staff into the ground to mark the boundary and the staff at once grew and burst into bloom 'ever on the feast of the Nativity, when, amid the snows of winter, every other branch is bare of leaf and blossom'.

After hearing this story, an infirmarian called Oswald determined to buy a holy thorn tree for the garden in which he grew special herbs to help cure the sick and elderly. Finding such a tree was a difficult task, however. The monks at Glastonbury who had lost their once highly profitable relics in a fire in 1184, had traded for centuries on the legend of the holy tree. They did not intend to lose their revenue from pilgrims who visited the tree by admitting or allowing the existence of a Christmas-flowering tree elsewhere.

Oswald eventually obtained a small packet of seeds of the thorn tree from a traveller who claimed to have passed through Glastonbury, but although some of the seeds did produce shoots, they looked no different after several years from wild hawthorn and blossomed in much the same way.

'You'll need to take a cutting or two from the holy tree, which you must then graft on to one growing in the wild,' the abbey's monk-gardener told him. 'I shall be visiting the place soon to help them plant an orchard, and I'll see what I can do for you.'

A month later, the gardener brought Oswald half a dozen short sticks which, he claimed, were from the holy tree itself. Two years later, having been grafted on to the wild stock, three sticks began to bud during November and on 5 January, the old

Christmas Eve, one stick burst into bloom.

Brother Oswald kept the matter to himself, for he had no wish to reveal to the abbot that he had been a receiver of what might have been regarded as stolen goods, however holy they might be. Also, he had no desire to see thousands of local pilgrims trampling down his carefully tilled and manured soil every Christmastide. He had an even stronger reason for silence, however: he was not sure what others called 'the mystic thorn' really was as blessed as the monks from Glastonbury Abbey claimed. He did not discount the value of miracles, for they did encourage visitors, both rich and poor alike, to donate money generously, but as a practical man, he had his personal doubts.

THE WHITE THORN TREE

William Turner, Dean of Wells and the father of English botany, wrote in his New Herball of 1562:

In Summerstershyre about six myles from Welles, in ye park of Glassenbury there is a hawthorne which is grene all the wynter, as all they that dwell there about do stedfastly holde.

Just thirty-five years later, the noted herbalist John Gerard reported:

. . . of the White Thorne, or Hawthorne tree, we have in the West of England one growing at a place called Glastonbury, which bringeth forth flowers about Christmas by the report of divers of good credit who have seen the same; but myself have not seen it, and therefore leave it to be better examined.

In 1735 Philip Miller pointed out in his *Gardening Dictionary* that the Glastonbury thorn tree

is preserve'd in many Gardens as a Curiosity; this often produces some Bunches of Flowers in Winter, and afterwards flowers again at the Season with the common Sort, but doth in no other respect differ from the common Hawthorn.

The reason for the Christmas blossoming, he surmised, as other gardeners have done after him, was that the holy thorn tree was no ordinary English hawthorn but a tree from the warm countries of the East. If this were the case, then the tree would blossom at the same time as others of its species, which would be summer in the East and winter in the West. If, in fact, the original tree had been planted by St Joseph – Oswald disbelieved the story that the stake had taken root – then it would have come from a warm, distant land.

But although Brother Oswald might not have been impressed by the legend of the miraculous tree, others were and the admirers included some of the highest in the land. Thomas Cromwell was 'delighted' to receive blossoms. Elizabeth I showed considerable interest. Anne of Denmark, consort to James I, was reported to have paid 'large sums' for cuttings.

Many stories exist regarding monks and the founders of religious houses which bear their name and much pleasure can be gained from searching for them in old books and manuscripts. The legend of St Albans, the great Benedictine monastery in Hertfordshire, dates to the third century when the Christian faith was not tolerated.

Alban, a learned and brave man, gave shelter to a priest, then donned the stranger's clothes and surrendered to the soldiers. Even under severe torture he would not betray his faith and eventually he was taken for execution to 'a most pleasant spot covered with bushes and flowers'. He fell on his knees and prayed for water and 'immediately a living spring broke out before his feet, in which he quenched his thirst'.

Alban had displayed compassion for his fellow man even on the way to his execution. The 'great multitude' following him would not cross a narrow bridge, so the saint prayed for a moment on the river bank. The waters 'miraculously divided, and as many as a thousand persons passed dry-shod'.

According to the chronicler the Venerable Bede, the people built a church of wonderful workmanship in the place where the miracle had occurred. However, in the subsequent wars and ravages of pagan nations the memory of the martyr had almost perished and the place of his burial was forgotten until a miracle occurred in AD 793.

The legend of St Albans, the great Benedictine monastery in Hertfordshire

Offa, King of the Mercians, was advised by an angel from heaven that the remains of St Alban should be disinterred so that the saint could be venerated. King Offa came to Verulam and there they found the body of St Alban lying in a wooden coffin; the pious king immediately founded a church and in its vicinity arose the great Benedictine monastery and the town of St Albans in Hertfordshire.

Legends, holy relics and miracles did much to increase the wealth of monasteries during the early Middle Ages and they were an important source of income even after the Norman Conquest of England instigated the building of many new monasteries.

After 1066, the new nobility and moneyed classes began founding abbeys and priories throughout this country, endowing them with thousands of acres of their lands. The prime condition to each endowment was that the community would pray in perpetuity for the salvation of the founders' souls and those of their ancestors and heirs. Because it was believed that only the most generous offerings would reap salvation in heaven, the rich benefactors financed the building of religious institutions with zeal.

It was important for those monasteries with wealthy and generous founders and patrons to treat their new providers with respect. This lesson was learnt by a monk from a northern house to his chagrin. By nature the monk was not a rude man – in fact, no one had ever seen him lose his temper without first having been sorely provoked. However, when one bright June morning he discovered that, in the little garden behind the stables where the junior monks relaxed and occasionally played bowls, the roses had been picked, he swore vehemently. Such an offence would not have been deemed great and would have been punished by the withdrawal of the monk's beer for a week and banishment to a remote grange, with hard farm labour for a second offence. In this instance, however, the monk's blasphemy had been heard by two genteel ladies who were, in fact, near-relatives of the founder of the abbey and patrons of the institution.

'But . . . but the roses . . .' the monk stammered. 'They had picked the roses I had been growing for the sacrist to put on the altar and around the church.'

'And does that entitle you to vent your wrath?' asked the abbot. 'Your only excuse – and it is a fragile one – is that three days ago I gave those ladies full rights to the garden. I should have told you, I quite forgot.'

The monk's protestations were silenced by the abbot. Patrons, he explained, were special people with special rights who could exercise a profound influence on everything that happened within the house and, indeed, the church if their benefactions were sufficiently large. These rights could be passed down through families and even bequeathed.

Sometimes the influence of patrons was welcome, for they could expedite the business of the religious house in the royal courts and bring a favourable view to bear on matters affecting the abbey's own rights to land, fisheries, forests, and so on. Many patrons – and the ladies were such – gave generously to safeguard the financial interest of houses in their patronage.

The ladies had asked for a garden with roses and their request had been granted. The monk, as gardener, had been given the task of caring for it. It was agreed that the ladies would come only once a year, having made arrangements for their visit in advance, and they would expect to pick only the finest blooms from what was now their plot.

The monk found the question of patronage irksome, particularly when it concerned the intru-

sion of his garden and he expressed his views to the sacristan. The reply he received was that he had come into the world with nothing and would leave it with nothing. A monk, he was reminded, possessed nothing, for his soul belonged to the Almighty and his mind and body were for all time at the abbot's command.

Later that year, when visiting the garden of a monk he had met at a fair and who had promised him cuttings of blackberries that had been taken from the wild and were growing now without thorns and with large purple fruits, he learned that the founders of abbeys expected favours of a spiritual as well as material nature in return for their patronage.

The most important requirement of patrons was their first claim on the prayers of the community every day of the year. Furthermore, they expected the monks' prayers even after their death. The executors of the Earl of Oxford, for example, were required by his will to arrange for the saying of two thousand masses in the several religious houses that he had founded. A general requirement by important founders of religious houses such as kings and other royal persons was for their successors to be solemnly installed as patrons in the abbey church with all the ceremonies due to a bishop. Founders and their successors were invariably allocated rooms for themselves and for their families and even, in some cases, gardens of their own and free board whenever they visited the area. Most well-founded monasteries contained a founder's lodging, often of considerable size, in which he and his family resided for long periods.

Most founders took full advantage of the many benefits of patronising a monastery. The Earl of Oxford, for example, moved with his retinue and family from one of his foundations to another, spending part of the summer in one institution and a few months of the winter in another.

The Duke of Suffolk and his wife, Queen Mary, sister of Henry VIII and dowager of France, would spend weeks in the great Augustinian house of Butley, near Ipswich. To the consternation of the brethren, who had few contacts with the opposite sex, Mary even arranged picnic suppers in the canons' gardens during the hot weather.

Patrons had the right of burial in the choir and

a right to the display of arms, as may be seen over the great gate at Kirkham Priory and elsewhere. The body of King John, founder of Worcester Abbey, lies before the high altar of the cathedral and the remains of Edward II are similarly placed in Gloucester Cathedral. At Tewkesbury, tombs of the Clare family are ranged around the high altar of the abbey; the figures that hang high above are portraits of founders and not of saints. At Lanercost in Cumberland the arms of the Scrope family were embroidered on a cope.

Among the favours that founders expected from the monasteries was the preparation of long and not often strictly accurate genealogies to enhance their family lineage.

About seven hundred new monasteries were built during the following century, but some institutions were unable to provide sufficient income to keep their communities alive. Even the well-endowed houses often lacked the business skills and trading experience to survive and often found themselves heavily in debt.

Monasteries initially gained revenue from many sources, shrines and relics with a reputation for producing miracles providing a good source of income. Thus, the Glastonbury thorn tree was much visited by the credulous, to the obvious profit of the monks. Elsewhere, saints, relics and holy places were exploited by ambitious abbots. Most monasteries had a particular relic or shrine

for pilgrims to pray before – and what could not be authenticated was nevertheless displayed.

Tombs such as that of St Thomas à Becket at Canterbury gave men and women hope of a cure of spiritual and bodily ills. The visit itself – with a suitable donation to the religious institution – was often considered enough to ensure a safe passage to heaven. At Boxley, near Maidstone, one cynic wrote of an image there that contained 'certain engines and old wires with old rotten sticks at the back of the same which caused the eyes to wink'.

When pilgrimages were at their most popular, queues formed to see the Blood of Hailes, the bell of St Guthlac at Ripton Priory which it was said cured diseases of the head, the skull of St Petronilla at Bury St Edmunds which dispelled fevers, and the image of St Bride at Arden which either recovered lost cows or healed them.

Other popular pilgrimages were to Simon de Montfort's foot at Alnwick Abbey, Thomas of Lancaster's felt hat at Pontefract and the taper at Cardigan which, it was claimed, burned in that house without being consumed. The image of Darvell Gatheren, which was of such power that it could stop Welshmen from going to hell, was also popular, as was the bearded St Uncumber at St Paul's Cathedral, London. Such pilgrimages were later to be condemned by Cromwell and others and it was a Roundhead who took an axe to the Glastonbury thorn tree and cut it down.

However, the relics of saints and the promise of miracles were not the only sources of monastic income. At Leonard's Priory, Stamford, for example, the monks were clearly involved in the perfume, chemistry or even alchemy business, for excavations have revealed a drain that was filled in the late fifteenth century with glass-distilling vessels, crucibles and mercury. Similar material has been found at the monasteries of Pontefract and Selborne.

Copying and illuminating work became another source of income. At Mount Grace, where each member of the Carthusian community had his own small cell and individual garden, a successful printing operation existed before the dissolution of the monasteries. At Tavistock, the monks earned their income from a sophisticated printing venture and from the tin mines. In 1534 they combined both

There were many sources of income within the monastery

activities by printing the statutes of the tinners' parliament.

Some nunneries earned money by offering accommodation, but their lodgers sometimes became a nuisance. At Gracedieu in 1440, the bishop ordered the removal of a Frenchwoman 'because of the unseemliness of her life, for she received all alike to her embraces'; the nunnery of Legbourne was plagued by a 'secular woman who lies of night in the dorter among the nuns, bringing with her birds, by whose twittering silence is broken and the rest of the nuns disturbed'. Another lady lodger 'attended church with twelve dogs which make a great uproar'.

Students would pay to stay at the monasteries, a further source of income. These pupils were often the scions of noblemen or gentlemen and were called 'commensales' of the abbot's table. Often, however, the abbot was made to wait for his fees. The assistant of the Prior of West Acre in Norfolk wrote in 1494:

> 'There are many boys, sons of gentlemen, in the house, but the prior can't get their money to pay for their board and tuition.'

At this time, of course, Eton and Winchester were still taking in only poor and destitute youngsters.

A common tactic when financial disaster loomed was to sell corrodies, by which an abbot undertook to provide lodging, food, drink and even clothing for a lump sum paid in advance. As few of those selling corrodies were skilled in financial matters, they rarely counted the total cost and consequently often struck bad bargains.

The monastery at Durham owned coal mines at Ferryhill and Gateshead, with the right of timber for the pits and water-gate. Finchdale church had a coal mine in 1486 with a pumping station worked by a horse. In the twelfth century, the religious institutions of St Bees and Byland were mining for iron, much of it finding its way to the four forges of Kirkstead for smelting and the two for working iron fuel.

Lead was vital in the building of monasteries and houses. Fountains Abbey, which was built in close proximity to lead-mines, quickly turned an unexpected inheritance to profit. The mines, which had been worked by the Romans a thousand years before the foundations of the monastery were laid, may have been worked by the Britons even before the Romans. The monks had full mineral rights in the district and established a large smelting works at Smelthouse. So great was their activity, one chronicler reported, that in meeting the prodigious charcoal requirements they cut down completely the great forest of Knaresborough.

Many monasteries owned saltpits and several had rights to take ferm for glass-making. St Albans had a fulling mill for processing yarn and compelled all weavers of the town to use it. Meaux Abbey had a tannery where the monks kept a store of 'cow and calf leather, sole peces, sclepe, chowtheyds and wambes', plus tubs, tools and tan from the oaks that were barked during each year.

The wealthy community of monks at Glastonbury invested income in town lands and built up its holdings in London and Bristol considerably before the mid-fifteenth century. In London, the dean and chapter of St Paul's and the prior of Lewes began shop-row developments. The dean and chapter of Exeter Cathedral in 1394–5 rebuilt for leasing a newly acquired high street tenement. The abbot of Tewkesbury built a terrace of twenty-four cottages, presumably available for letting. The cannons of Walsingham built a chapel to enclose the famous shrine that was so popular for pilgrimages.

All these activities, however, earned only a small income when compared with the development of the land. The Cistercians were particularly skilled in this respect and one historian remarked that in some ways the Cistercians were better gardeners and farmers than they were monks. This comment may not have been fair, but another critic commented that they cleared wastes and transformed the desert-like surroundings of their abbeys.

> Meadow appeared in place of moorland; arable land replaced the heath and gorse-encumbered uplands. They planted woods and coppices; they directed water-courses; they made bridges and roads. They introduced new methods and new seed. Travelling in France and Italy, they kept their eyes and ears open during foreign wanderings and brought back new ideas, fresh knowledge, to add to the common stock.

The Cistercians built up herds of cattle and droves of horses and one abbey alone, that of Meaux, is reported to have possessed landed properties in well over one hundred different places, many of them in the neighbourhood of the abbey. The monks at several Yorkshire monasteries became notable horse breeders and it is said that many of the fine race-horses of our time may have sprung from stock which flourished on the Yorkshire moors.

However, the Cistercians, will be remembered most for their success in breeding and raising sheep. Towards the end of the twelfth century, the Cistercians were among the country's leading producers of wool and they continued to be so for many years. Two centuries later, the wool staple had become the principal trade of the country.

The Cistercians' success as breeders of sheep was a happy accident. The habit that the Cistercian order adopted was of white wool and originally the monks kept sheep to provide them with the material to make their garments. Gradually, their flocks began to increase among the northern grasslands and heather, and the monks discovered that the number of their sheep were increasing faster than those of landowners and other religious houses in the south. With the commercial acumen for which they were noted, the Cistercians began dealing with the wool merchants who were desperate to meet the growing demands of the Flemish cloth industry.

The Cistercians' success in rearing sheep was aided by the way in which their community was run: the small outlying communities were housed in granges; enormous areas of waste and unoccupied land were available to the monks and they were dedicated to work rather than to study (no Cistercian was allowed to carry a book). In the next century, Cistercian abbeys were exporting fleeces and wool to Italy and the Netherlands and for a time they were making more profits than the major commercial graziers throughout the country.

Medieval tools were heavy and cumbersome

Monastic orders transformed the barren landscape

ENCLOSING THE GARDEN

A monastery garden was often described as an enclosed garden (hortus conclusus). In those days the garden was enclosed for two reasons.

1. Vagabonds who roamed around the country, existing on whatever food they could find, would have known monastery gardens were a valuable source of fruit and vegetables. The monk gardener had also to protect his coleworts and lettuce from hungry rabbits and other four legged predators. A wattle fence would have helped to protect delicate plants from damaging cold winds and afforded a welcome shade from the sun when temperatures soared into heatwave conditions.

2. There would have been a reassuring sense of peace and security within the monastery walls. The monks could then walk undisturbed through the gardens enjoying the singing of the birds and the murmur of water trickling through the fountains. They could pause for a while by the fishponds admiring the carp, and pick an aromatic sprig of thyme or marjoram enjoying the pleasant scents released through the warmth of their fingers.

The Wattle Fence

This was a popular and perhaps the most economical method of enclosing the garden. At Westminster Abbey willow cuttings from the osier beds by the River Thames found a ready market and were often used for making fences. Today a wattle fence can give shade in a small garden, add an historical interest or just make an attractive feature.

The best time to build a wattle fence is in the spring when willow, hazel, holly and other indigenous branches are pliable and easy to handle.

To make a fence 4ft (120cm) high take stakes 4ft 6ins (135cm) long and hammer them 6ins (15cm) into the ground. Tread the soil around the stakes so that they are firmly fixed, then take pliable branches of willow, hazel, ivy or other creepers and weave between the upright stakes. Tie where necessary with raffia or binder twine. A little practice will soon result in a neat finish. This type of fencing will not last for more than a few years, but results are immediate and given an established look to a newly planted garden.

The Emperor's Plants

Long before the Norman Conquest of Britain, Charlemagne, King of the Franks and Emperor of the Holy Roman Empire, who reigned from 800 to 814, wrote a plant list that was to influence monk-gardeners from the ninth century to the present day.

Charlemagne was dedicated more to the creation of peace and stability than to the making of beautiful gardens, but he believed that if the warring nations who were under his rule could be introduced to the hoe and spade, they might become more peace-loving. He issued a decree that each of his many properties in all the cities throughout the empire should have a garden and they were given a list of a hundred herbs and fruit-bearing trees to plant.

This list, dated 872, is remarkable because of its practicality. Earlier writers had confined themselves to herbs and exotic plants, but Charlemagne listed those he considered to be useful in the kitchen as well as for decorative and medicinal purposes.

Historians have for long debated the question of who advised the emperor on what plants he should include in his list. Several names have been suggested, but in the authors' opinion the most likely is a former pupil of the cathedral school of York, a boy called Alcuin who eventually became abbot of the influential monastery of St Martin at Tours, France.

Alcuin was a keen amateur botanist and plant hunter and, after leaving school in 753, he travelled extensively seeking out plants, gardens and manuscripts. He rejoined the school as a master, but soon tired of the bad weather

GARDENING MONKS AND CLERICS

Few abbots of Cistercian monasteries would have shown any great interest in books, for when not in church monks of the Order were expected to be out and about in the gardens, fields, granges and workshops. No man – sat with folded hands – in a Cistercian house; he was at the plough, grinding corn at the mill, shearing sheep at the granges, fashioning ironwork at the smithy, melting ore at the forge, winning lead from the mines, cutting wood in the forests.

The bookworms were the Benedictines. They had always been devoted to the study and love of books. Many writers on horticulture were monk gardeners or connected in some way with the religious movement. Walafrid Strabo (his surname meant squint eye) was a monk at the island monastery of Reichenau near Lake Constance, just a ride away from St. Gall. His philosophy is summed up thus.

Though a life of retreat offers various joys,
None, I think, will compare with the time one employs
In the study of herbs, or in striving to gain
Some practical knowledge of nature's domain.
Get a garden! What kind you get matters not.

In his Hortulus (The Little Garden), Strabo mentions 29 plants he knew and obviously loved. His manuscript lay undisturbed among the papers of St. Gall until 1624, although it would have been read by soil loving monks many centuries earlier.

The discoverer seemed to believe in the phrase 'finders' keepers', for he took Strabo's manuscript with him and it was not until 1922 that it was translated – from a copy. In 1966 Raef Payne translated it again most beautifully into hexameters.

With other monks, Strabo would probably have read An Inquiry into Plants by Theophrastus, who studied under Aristotle and inherited the great man's garden and collection of texts. His beliefs were regarded as strange, even for the time, but his stories of Alexander the Great's specially trained observers on their expeditions into Asia, and of the plants they found there, would have been riveting stuff for cloistered monks.

Strabo died in 849 AD at the age of 40, while fording a river. One of his last pieces of verse was about sage, which he considered had a justifiable reputation for prolonging life. He wrote that it deserved to grow green, 'forever enjoying perpetual youth'.

As might have been expected, many of the writers gave their attention to herbs. These little plants had been admired and their powers respected for centuries. Alcuin, a garden-loving monk of the Benedictine Order and former master in the cathedral school in York, asked in Charlemagne's court 'What is a herb?' The Emperor had a ready response. 'A herb,' he answered, 'is the friend of physicians and the praise of cooks.'

Many monks would have had access to a herbal written in Greek and translated into Latin by Apuleius Platonicus about 420 BC. Those walking and resting under the shade of the olive trees in the gardens of Monte Cassino liked it enough to make copies, one of which ended up in the library of the abbey of Bury St. Edmunds. Here, in 1120, the English monks translated it into Anglo-Saxon.

and yearned for the flowers, vines and fruits of sunnier climes. Charlemagne befriended him and soon emperor and scholar found themselves discussing the subject both enjoyed the most – gardens and gardening. It is probable that, during his stay in Charlemagne's court, Alcuin put forward his grand plan to organise the planting of beautiful and useful gardens throughout the empire.

Some chroniclers, however, attribute Charlemagne's list to the great gardener Benedict who belonged to the monastery at Aniane, who not only discussed plants and planting with the emperor but exchanged cuttings and roots as well.

Although several other names have been suggested, Alcuin's name is not among them. The reason that the authors favour him is that, according to records, Alcuin decorated his room at the monastery with his favourite

Alcuin preparing plans for gardens throughout the empire

flowers, lilies and roses. Coincidentally, the two plants that headed the emperor's list of plants were lilies and roses. It seems reasonable to believe that either Alcuin himself listed them first or Charlemagne placed them there as a gesture of friendship and gratitude.

Gardens were a feature of many monasteries and other religious houses, but evidence of their nature and purpose has been difficult to find. One of the best points of reference is a garden that, so far as is known, was never created. The garden is shown in a ninth-century plan for an ideal monastic community which was addressed to Abbot Gozbert of that monastery and dated just a few years after Charlemagne's death in 814. The plan outlines all the principal buildings, together with the lay-out and planting of gardens and an orchard. It is not known who drew up the plan, but most chroniclers suggest that it was Abbot Haito of Reichenau, an island monastery hardly a day's ride away from St Gall. Haito was a keen gardener who probably studied Charlemagne's list of plants. Other chroniclers, however, contend that the gardening-abbot Benedict originated the plan, but it may even have been Alcuin, for he was an avid collector of manuscripts and a keen researcher of gardening lore. He may have worked on the plan and left it with his papers which were discovered a few years after his death in 804. Perhaps all the monk-gardeners assembled together with the emperor and shared their knowledge and experience. Sadly, we may never know.

What we do know is that the St Gall plan is no rough sketch by an amateur artist. The man who drew up this plan was clearly a gardener, or at least a garden lover able and willing to take professional advice. He knew a great deal about vegetables, had more than a passing knowledge of the ways of poultry and was not squeamish about dung. Medicinal herbs held few secrets for him and he respected the sanctity of the graveyard.

In the plan, the church and cloister garden stand firmly at the centre. About a quarter of the site, running from south to north, is occupied with domestic food production and the medical work of the monastery. There are circular enclosures for ducks and geese, a hut for the fowl-keepers,

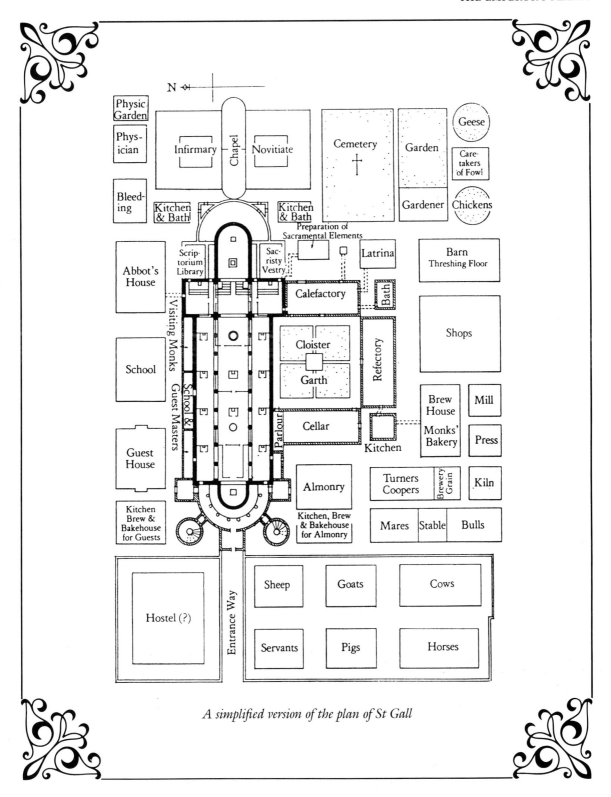

N

Physic Garden

Physician

Bleeding

Kitchen & Bath

Infirmary

Chapel

Novitiate

Cemetery

Garden

Geese

Caretakers of Fowl

Gardener

Chickens

Kitchen & Bath

Preparation of Sacramental Elements

Scriptorium Library

Sacristy Vestry

Latrina

Barn
Threshing Floor

Abbot's House

Visiting Monks

School & Guest Masters

Calefactory

Bath

Shops

School

Cloister

Garth

Refectory

Guest House

Parlour

Cellar

Brew House

Monks' Bakery

Mill

Press

Kitchen

Almonry

Turners Coopers

Brewery Grain

Kiln

Kitchen Brew & Bakehouse for Guests

Kitchen, Brew & Bakehouse for Almonry

Mares

Stable

Bulls

Hostel (?)

Entrance Way

Sheep

Goats

Cows

Servants

Pigs

Horses

A simplified version of the plan of St Gall

Lettuce

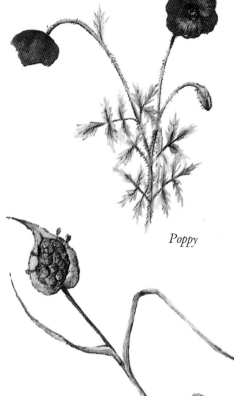

Poppy

Garlic

a house for the gardener and a garden of herbs with eighteen plots, one for each variety of plant. This neat grouping is adjacent to the monks' cemetery, which also doubles as an orchard. Next comes the convent for the novices and the infirmary, alongside which are the physic garden, a house for the doctor, a blood-letting chamber and two bathing places.

Running east to west on the south side of the monastic complex there is a barn – a collective workshop probably intended for housing benches with knife-grinding and maintenance tools – and areas for the millers, the mortar mixers, the potters at their kilns, the coopers, the wheelwrights and the general workmen.

There is stabling for horses and oxen, with chambers for their keepers, and an interesting group of buildings for sheep and shepherds, goats and goatherds, cows and cowherds, swine and swineherds, brood mares with their foals and keepers, and for servants from outlying estates.

A kitchen with a hospice for pilgrims and paupers is set near the main gate. Brewing and baking chambers are linked to the kitchen, which in turn has a passageway to a very large larder and the refectory. The cloisters and dormitory are positioned alongside the church, with the catering arrangements close at hand.

On the north side there is a further kitchen, a guesthouse, a school, a chamber for the abbot and a place for servants. In their three-volume interpretation of the plan, architects Walter Horn and Ernest Born refer to the clever way in which the planners placed the vegetable garden between the orchard and the poultry runs and in close proximity to the monks' routine. As the architects point out, the garden would have drawn the most effective fertiliser from the nitrogen-rich droppings of the nearby fowl yards. Another source of fertiliser would have been the monks' privy, particularly if the design allowed for waste to be gathered in settling tanks.

With the mills, brewing and baking areas in close proximity, grain feed for the chickens and geese would have been on hand. Furthermore, this food could have been augmented by trimmings from the vegetables and by fallen fruit from the orchard.

The ninth-century planner left nothing to chance. In the plan, he indicates not just where the gardener is to live but what he is to grow. Over his drawing of the eighteen plots which form the kitchen garden, he has entered the name of the variety of plant each plot is to contain.

Plots one to nine are reserved for onion, leek, celery, coriander, dill, poppy, radish, another variety of poppy and chard. On plots ten to eighteen, the gardener is advised to grow garlic, shallot, parsley, chervil, lettuce, pepperwort, parsnip, cabbage and fennel. These are clearly seasonings or spices to flavour the monks' vegetable diet. The lay-out leaves two presumptions to be made. One is that some form of crop rotation would have been ventured in later years. Another is that, as no root crops such as beet and turnip are indicated, these would have grown on land on the other side of the monastery walls.

Thirteen planting areas for trees and fourteen areas for graves are indicated, a large cross being drawn in the centre of the oblong orchard. Seven of the burial plots are placed east of the cross, five to the west and two in the central area. The numbers thirteen and fourteen (twice seven) are regarded as important here, for both were sacred numbers. Thirteen apostles attended the last supper with Christ. Seven was a favourite number of St Augustus who wrote that it expressed the wholeness and completeness of all created things. As other authorities have suggested, the number seven was traditionally believed to order all

Corriander

Radish

Dill

human life. There were seven capital sins, seven virtues and seven daily services in the church.

In this blue-print for the ideal monastery, seven buildings formed the cloister and seven steps connected the pathways. The lay-out of this area has for long fascinated gardeners with an interest in mathematics and readers might care to follow the argument of the interpreters of the plan regarding the use of sacred numbers. The width of the plots is 6¼ft (190cm) (composed of two standard 2½ft (76cm) modules with one 1¼ft (40cm) submodule). Their length, 17½ft (533cm), reflects again the number seven: $7 \times 2\frac{1}{2} = 17\frac{1}{2}$.

Horn and Born write:

> Thus, in each plot the bodies of seven brothers could be accommodated, in keeping with the application of standard modules to achieve the human scale of the other facilities of the plan. And as elsewhere, this compounding and multiplication of sevens can hardly be fortuitous, but on the contrary, quite purposeful in the planning of the cemetery.

In designing the medicinal garden, the ninth-century planner has abandoned the use of sacred numbers. There are sixteen plots which contain kidney bean, savory, rose, watercress, cumin, lovage, fennel, tansy, white lily, sage, rue, cornflag, pennyroyal, fenugreek, peppermint and rosemary.

A unique feature of the plan is the house for blood-letting. Bleeding was an essential part of the monastic routine, but no other records show a house being especially designed for the purpose.

Charlemagne's influence over garden design and planting was matched by his desire to civilise and unify the nations which fell under his domain. As the first Christian emperor of the West and a strong advocate of monasticism, he saw a solution to his problems in the rule of life laid down by St Benedict, who had died at the abbey of Monte Cassino over three hundred years earlier. Charlemagne decreed that all monks within his empire should follow the Benedictine Rule and that they should use it to lead the heathens of his domain to salvation.

BENEDICT AND HIS RULE OF LIFE

During his first year as a pupil gardener, a young monk called Phillip gained a valuable and unforgettable insight into the history and workings of the rule that governed the monastic way of life.

One day when Phillip was sowing seeds of colewort for the kitchens, a large crow fluttered to his feet and began to make a plaintive call. Surprised, Phillip waved his hoe at the bird to frighten it, but the crow came nearer and squawked louder, attracting the attention of other monks working nearby. Phillip shook his hoe with even greater vigour and then let it drop to his side as the bird came almost to his feet and rested there, looking up with such trust that Phillip felt inclined to pick it up. Instead, he drew from inside his habit a small portion of bread that he had saved from his meal to stave off the pangs of hunger he felt at night. There was silence throughout the vegetable garden as the pupil monks and their seniors interrupted their work to see better what would happen next. Phillip fingered the bread for a moment and then dropped it to the ground; in the same instant the bird seized the bread and flew away with it in his beak.

Phillip's offence, as was made clear to him later that day by the prior, was serious. Food not eaten at mealtime was to be left to be gathered for the poor. To waste it by throwing even a crumb to a wild creature when men, women and children were begging at the gate was sufficiently serious for the abbot and the monastery officials to consider the next morning.

That evening and night and well into the following morning, the monk wondered at the penalty that was to be exacted. He had heard of brethren being whipped, put into dark cellars and fed once a day with a loaf of bread that was lowered on a cord, or cast out from the community and never allowed to return. To his surprise, however, and to the bewilderment of members of the community not privy to that morning's debate in the chapter house, Phillip was not punished. There was

an even greater surprise for the community that evening when the kitchener let it be known that as a special concession, or pittance, each member would receive an additional portion of bread.

The young novices had heard of pittances – ie, additional allowances of food – only in connection with saints' days or visits to the monastery by an important lord or bishop. They expected protests from the choir monks, for whom shortage of food at Lent was an essential part of the regime, but no murmurings in opposition occurred and Phillip was perplexed to see that even the sternest monks looked kindly towards him. The cellarer, second only to the abbot in importance, personally broke the loaves into pieces.

The crow visited Phillip in the garden the next day. Once again, those working nearby observed the scene. On this occasion, however, the bird did not beg for food. It simply picked a worm from a clod of soil near the young man's feet and fluttered away.

Unlike the day before, the senior monks who had left their work elsewhere to visit the garden began to talk among themselves, breaking the silence that had ruled in the garden for a decade. They watched intently as the young monk pushed his hoe backwards and forwards over the soil. However, he was not concerned about being the object of so much attention. Rather, his thoughts were on the short phrase uttered by several senior monks: 'Just like St Benedict,' they had cried. 'Just like St Benedict.'

That evening, as the community began the repast of the day, they broke with tradition. It was the custom for one of the senior monks to read aloud from the scriptures. On this occasion, however, it was not a monk from the choir who mounted the short flight of steps to the lectern, but the abbot himself. With the complete attention of the monks, the abbot spoke for fifteen minutes.

Benedict, the community learned, had himself saved some of his ration of bread to feed a crow, which visited him every day, and it was a crow which had snatched from the saint's hand a poisoned loaf he had been given to eat by those opposed to his reforming ways and obedience to God.

Benedict, the abbot explained, was the father of monks. It was he who, after working daily in the garden of the famous abbey of Monte Cassino, wrote a set of regulations, now called the Rule, for all who desired to devote their lives to God.

'So you see,' the novice master said to Phillip later, in the short period when talk was permitted, 'that business with the crow slighly unnerved everyone. There were some who talked in terms of a miracle and reincarnation, but the majority saw it as an important reminder to us all that the spirit of Benedict is with us and that the rule must be observed.'

The Rule was intended by Benedict to help ordinary persons to follow a way of life which would lead them to salvation. Benedict's ideas were completely new, for he underlined the need for work for everyone – whether they were rich or poor – who sought God. Benedict believed that work was as important to the Christian's well-being as prayer and that to work was the natural condition of man. Therefore, to carry out such tasks as cultivating a garden, tending pigs, building a barn, illuminating a manuscript and caring for the sick was as essential to those adopting the monastic way of life as

St Benedict (from an engraving by Wierx)

it was for them to say matins at daybreak and to sing mass at noon.

During the following months, Phillip gathered together the details of Benedict's life and how, at the age of nineteen, he had left his luxurious Roman home at Nursia in Italy to join a religious community in the mountains many miles away. Later he lived as a hermit in a cave at Subiaco, clad only in a habit given to him by the abbot of a nearby monastery and sustained with bread that was lowered to him from a rock above by monks who were much moved, as were others, by his humble demeanour and dedication.

There were times, however, when Benedict's mind was filled with thoughts of the beautiful girl he had left behind in Nursia and he confessed later to suffering agonies of the flesh. One day, when the torture was more than he could bear, he threw himself naked into a thicket of thorns at the cave's entrance and rolled in it until his flesh was torn and his desires were subdued. Francis of Assisi, who in 1209 founded the Franciscan order, planted two rose bushes near the thorns in recognition of the saint. Some declared that Francis simply touched the thorns and they blossomed as roses, but Phillip preferred to think of the gentle man with his spade in his hand digging holes for the roses and taking care not to harm a single red worm or insect while he did so.

Benedict eventually relinquished his hermit's life and became an abbot of a monastery, but the community disregarded his counsel and in despair he returned to his cave. Soon Benedict had many disciples who sought to benefit from his wisdom and learning and within a few years the cave became the site of a monastery and twelve others were built around the valley. Benedict eventually joined the monks at Monte Cassino and it was here that he wrote his rule. He died in 544, aged 63, and he was buried in a grave which he had asked to have dug six days earlier.

Scribes at Monte Cassino made many copies of Benedict's Rule, but knowledge of it did not spread until a hundred years later, when the Lombards sacked the monastery. The dispossessed monks carried their copies of the rule to other monasteries throughout Italy and gradually the knowledge of it spread.

BISHOP'S MOVE

In the early thirteenth century, Bishop Geoffrey Ridel was hard at work on the building of Ely Cathedral's magnificent west front, and after some clandestine searching found just the oak trees he needed at Elmsett, which was within the territory of a rival builder, Abbot Samson of Bury St. Edmunds.

In a covert operation the bishop placed a secret mark on those he needed, then boldly asked Sanson's permission to have 'some of your trees' felled and carried away. The abbot was in no position to refuse, but when Ridel's men turned up a few days later they found that the best of the trees had gone and were already being prepared for use in the building of the great tower of Bury St. Edmunds, where they remain to this day.

St.Augustine meets Ethelbert and Bertha

It was St Augustine, a monk from a Roman monastery, who with companions first introduced the order of St Benedict into England during the seventh century. On their journey to England these chosen missionaries were seized, we are told, 'with a sudden fear, and began to think of returning home rather than proceed to a barbarous, fierce, unbelieving nation, to whose very language they were strangers'. They landed in the Isle of Thanet, in Kent, and were received graciously by the Saxon King Ethelbert and his Christian wife Bertha. With the king's permission, they entered the city of Canterbury, carrying the holy cross for all to see and singing hallelujah.

From the time of St Augustine, monasteries accepted the Rule of St Benedict and those which rose in England during the next six hundred years were chiefly founded by or for the members of this order. One chronicler wrote:

When we were only just emerging from barbarism, we find these munificent and energetic communities draining the marshes of Lincolnshire and Somersetshire, clearing the midland and northern forests, planting, building, and transcribing Bibles for the honour of God and the good of the poor; and though their cultivated fields and gardens, and their cloisters, churches, libraries and schools were laid waste, burned, and pillaged by the devastations of the Danes, yet the spirit in which they had worked survived, and their institutions were afterwards restored with more extensive means, and all the advantages afforded by improved skill in mechanical and agricultural science.

Canterbury Cathedral

The garden at Abbey House, Leeds

Abbots, Arbours
and
Flowery Meads

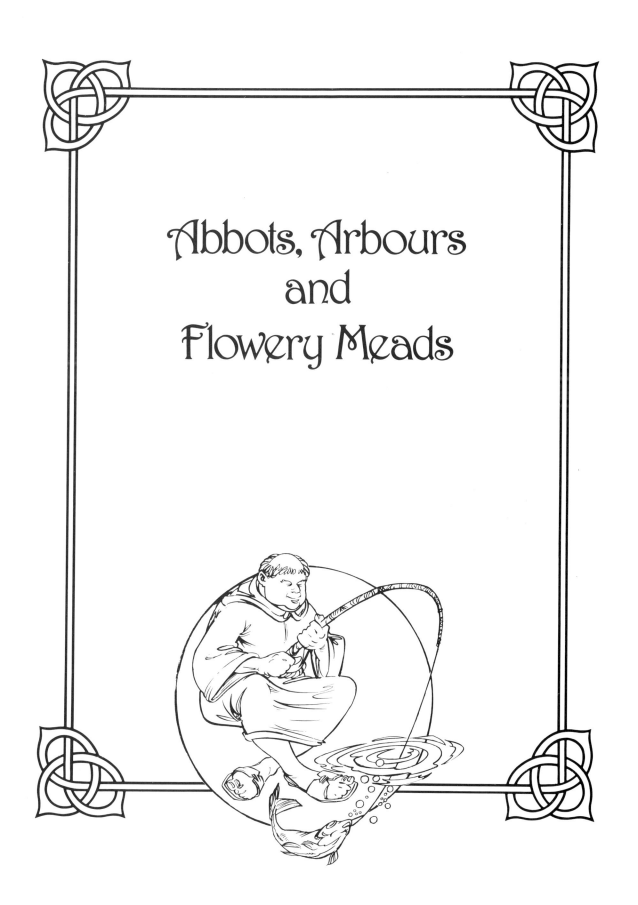

According to the light conversation that took place at one religious foundation, their much respected abbot had been conceived in an arbour of honeysuckle and born the following spring beneath a gooseberry bush. Nobody believed that, of course, for the Abbot John was an aristocrat on whose family fortune the brethren relied for essential rebuilding work, but no one doubted the fact that he did have an uncanny way of getting plants to flourish and a knowledge of grafting, pruning and taking cuttings that was unmatched. Even Brother Martin, for fifteen years a monk-gardener at the monastery and acknowledged master of the gardening craft, bowed to the master's expertise.

The abbot not only knew special ways of manuring apple trees so that they would produce more crops, but he was also a ready adviser on pest control. 'Caterpillars,' he told Martin, 'have been found among the coleworts you delivered to the kitchener yesterday afternoon. There is no need for caterpillars if you follow the advice of the Romans and go out in the early morning and pick the little wretches off by hand.'

'Alternatively,' he said loudly so that all the monks in the area could hear him, 'go out in the evening just before the sun goes down and the light fades and shake the vegetables thoroughly. The caterpillars will fall to the ground either to die of the night's cold or to be taken as food by our ever-present friends the birds. Do you heed

A corner of the garden at Michelham Priory

my advice, Brother Martin?'

Martin indicated that he did, and was about to begin hoeing again when Abbot John proposed another remedy. This was to prepare a mixture of olive oil, bitumen and sulphur, all boiled together, and to smear this around the stems of the plants.

'Against ants,' the abbot continued, 'smear the trunks of trees and bushes with a mixture of red earth and tar. This will prevent them from carrying off seeds and the tender parts of plants which they store in their nests against old age, just as the squirrels store nuts under stones and the hedgehogs build up fat in their systems.'

The abbot had another method for deterring ants. This was to hang a rotting fish from a branch. The ants were attracted to this and when the fish was covered in the insects, it would be cut down and fed to the chickens.

A 15th century watering device made of clay

The abbot, often pressed into service by the king as a diplomat, had seen for himself the great gardens of southern Europe and had sat with the nobility on seats of turf and fragrant chamomile under arbours of vines, roses and honeysuckle. He had plucked ripe peaches and apricots from trees that had been grown in basins and, while preparing to put forward the king's arguments, had wandered over lawns of a thousand flowers. When he returned, frequently carrying seeds, cuttings and plants, he became more determined each time to provide for himself gardens that offered the same sense of peace and harmony as those of Moorish Spain.

He planned to grow fruit trees, not because the fruits were required for the table but to delight the onlooker as the trees burst into blossom. He intended to plant aromatic shrubs and herbs, not to yield medicinal juices but to scent the air and to attract the colourful butterflies and bees. Flowers there would be, in abundance. And in the centre, scythed and rolled until it took on the appearance of a Persian carpet, would be the lawn.

Abbot John had an excellent guide to the art of making green swards of this nature. The guide was written by a Dominican monk, Albertus Magnus, who in 1260 had prepared a treatise on designing a pleasure garden and

how to make it. His work was copied by scribes in many monasteries and in 1471 it was printed.

Magnus advised that the gardener had first to prepare the ground. This he argued could

scarcely be done unless the roots are first dug out and the site levelled, and the whole well flooded with boiling water so that the fragments of roots and seeds remaining in the earth may not by any means sprout forth.

The plot was then to be covered with rich turf of flourishing grass, the turves beaten down with broad wooden mallets and the plants of grass trodden into the ground.

until they cannot be seen or scarcely anything of them perceived. For then little by little they may spring forth closely and cover the surface like a green cloth.

In this treatise, Magnus suggested that care had to be taken that the lawn was of such a size that 'about it in a square may be planted every sweet-smelling herb such as rue, and sage and basil, and likewise all sorts of flowers, as the violet, columbine, lily, rose, iris and the like.' He also advocated the making of 'a higher bench of turf flowering and lovely'. And he proposed that 'somewhere in the middle' there should be provision of seats 'so that men may sit down there to take their repose pleasurably when the senses need refreshment'. He continued:

Upon the lawn too, against the heat of the sun, trees should be planted or vines trained, so that the lawn may have a delightful and cooling shade, sheltered by their leaves. For from these trees shade is more sought after than fruit, so that not much trouble should be taken to dig about and manure them, for this might cause great damage to the turf.

Care should also be taken that the trees are not too close together or too numerous, for cutting off the breeze may do harm to health. The pleasure garden needs to have a free current of air along with shade. It

also needs to be considered that the trees should not
be bitter ones whose shade gives rise to diseases, such
as the walnut and some others; but let them be sweet
trees, with perfumed flowers and agreeable shade, like
grapevines, pears, apples, pomegranates, sweet bay
trees, cypresses and such like.

Behind the lawn there should be

great diversity of medicinal and scented herbs, not only
to delight the sense of smell by their perfume but to
refresh the sight with the variety of their flowers, and
to cause admiration at their many forms in those who
look at them.

Rue, Magnus said, should be set in many places 'for the
beauty of its green foliage and also that its biting quality
may drive away noxious vermin from the garden'. He
advised against the planting of trees in the middle of the
lawn. It was better, in his view, to let the surface of the
grass delight in the open air, for the air itself was then
more health-giving. Futhermore, if the lawn were to have
trees planted on it, spiders' webs stretched from branch
to branch would interrupt and entangle the faces of
passers-by.

On the siting of the garden, he proposed that it should
stand open to the north and east

since those winds bring health and cleanliness; to
the opposite winds of the south and west it should
be closed, on account of their turbulence bringing dirt
and disease; for although the north wind may delay the
fruit, yet it maintains the spirit and protects health. It
is then delight rather than fruit that is looked for in the
pleasure garden.

Magnus was much in favour of a clear fountain of water
in a stone basin 'for its purity gives much pleasure'.
Abbot John agreed wholeheartedly and had already
planned a series of surprises for those who would wander
there. The abbot was an admirer of Count Robert II of

Artois who loved water and built special engines which allowed him to play practical jokes on visitors. Unwelcome guests were dropped into a pile of feathers, soaked with jets of water from apparently innocent statues, had flour blown into their faces or were confronted with talking owls.

Another of the abbot's mentors was an Englishman, Bartholomew de Glanville, who wrote learnedly in 1240 on flowery meads. De Glanville believed that meads should be alive with herbs, grass and flowers. They should be fair, green, lovely to the sight 'and for sweet odour, they be liking to the smell, and feed the taste with savour of their herbs and of their grass'.

A further source of advice on garden design was the Andalusian Georgics, a rural poem composed in 1348. This suggested that a pleasure garden should be on a southern aspect with a walk or watercourse shaded by evergreens. There was to be a pavilion in the centre and varieties of flowers, trees and climbing vines.

After the moat had been dug and quick-thorns planted as a boundary, the abbot set to work on plans for the construction of covered and paved walks. He was anxious to include in his plant list the musk rose to add the atmosphere of the East to his new garden. There would also be aviaries for exotic birds, menageries of wild animals, fountains, waterfalls, lakes for colourful waterfowl, plantations of flowering trees and recreation areas for the playing of bowls and skittles.

Abbot John also intended to grow citrus fruits in the outbuildings, using steam to keep the plants warm. If this was successful, he would begin propagation of the double clove carnation, a flower that he particularly liked and which, to his certain knowledge, other gardening abbots had succeeded in cultivating in great numbers.

Abbot John was not an exception in being a gardener, for abbots had been planting gardens for centuries. Many had neither the benefit of expert advice nor the broadening experience of travel, but they were nevertheless successful gardeners.

An enthusiastic gardener was Eadfrith, Abbot of St Albans until 946. He spent much of his life as a hermit,

Madonna lily

caring for gardens of herbs and vegetables. It is believed that he also had a water garden. St Ethelwold, who in 966 commissioned the monk Godeman to write the now world-famous *Benedictional*, was also a garden lover. Ethelwold ensured that the splendid manuscript was well illustrated with flowers. One illustration depicted the madonna lily being held by St Etheldreda, head of the abbey she founded on the Isle of Eels (Ely) some three hundred years earlier.

Godeman, later to become abbot of Thorney, was also a gardener. He took over an abbey that was already becoming noted for its trees and natural beauty. In the twelfth century, William, abbot of Malmesbury, described

A quiet corner in a garden of today, specially planted to give the pleasant aroma of chosen herbs

it as 'set in a Paradise' with a multitude of trees. According to William, the level plain delighted the eye with its green grass. The ground was filled with apple-bearing trees and vines, which either crept along the ground or were supported on sticks. There was, William declared, a mutual struggle between nature and art.

The abbess of Romsey had flower gardens as early as 1092, for it was in that year that William Rufus and his courtiers asked to view the roses and other flowering herbs. His true intention, however, was to meet Edith of Scotland, the twelve-year-old heiress of the Saxon line, who was a boarder at the convent school.

At Bury St Edmunds a hundred years later, monks were busy in the cloisters using living plants as models for what is now known as the *Herbal of Apuleius*.

Cistercian abbots were probably inspired by the garden at Clairvaux, in Burgundy, the first daughter abbey of the order. William of Malmesbury reported a few years after the foundation of Clairvaux in 1115 that within the precinct there was a

> wide level area containing an orchard of many different fruit trees, like a little wood. Close by the infirmary, it is a great solace to the monks, a spacious promenade for those wishing to walk and a pleasing spot for those preferring to rest. At the end of the orchard a garden begins, divided into a number of beds by little canals which, though of still water, do flow slowly . . . the water thus serves a double purpose in sheltering the fish and irrigating the plants.

Until the dissolution of the monasteries in 1539, abbots spent time and money on their gardens. Richard Whiting, the last abbot of Glastonbury, talked in that year with Lord Stourton in an arbour of bay. Within months he was hanged on a gibbet on the Tor, a high mound overlooking the monastery and the gardens and orchard to which he and his predecessors had given much care.

Some sixty years earlier, Abbot John Selwood planted more than 3 acres of apples and pears 'of the finest fruit'. His successor, Richard Beere, fulfilled his gardening dreams at his manor at Meare by surrounding 3 acres with beautifully designed high walls. Within this he formed moats, dug pools and planted orchards. Meare, it is recorded, had other gardens, one of them extending for 2½ acres.

At Sharpham Park, near Glastonbury, the abbot enclosed 382 acres with sawn oak palings. Within the enclosure he planted an orchard and made new fish-ponds.

While pleasure gardens and flowery meads contributed little to the kitchens of the monastery, they did help the abbot to appear friendly or business-like to those of importance. Much business was done in such places as the bay arbour at Glastonbury, among the famous damson trees at Westminster and within some of the 40 acres of courtyards and rose gardens at the great abbey of Bury St Edmunds.

Talks could be concluded later over wine and fresh garden-grown strawberries in the abbot's ante-room. Patrons could be induced to provide additional income for the abbey, wool dealers could be persuaded to offer better terms and adjoining landowners could be cajoled into a more charitable mood when hunting, fishing and grazing rights were at issue.

Many visitors, such as abbots of other houses and dignitaries from overseas, were welcomed. From such visitors the abbot learned about events elsewhere and what action he should take to discourage more demands on his time and his treasury.

TRAVELLING MONKS

Not all abbots spent their time in their gardens and doing business in the cloisters, for many were great travellers and others had duties in government and the making of law. A few records exist that hint at the activities that took place when an abbot prepared for a journey to neighbouring monasteries or for a trip to Rome.

An abbot usually travelled in a primitive carriage, with a large team of horses, a mounted retinue of about twenty-four men and pack-horses. This made great demands on stabling and supplies so that provisioning was a major part of monastic life. In addition to the men who travelled with the abbot, others were sent ahead on horseback or in carts to help prepare for the arrival of the main party. An item of considerable importance was the 'horse bread' necessary for the riding and pack-horses.

An abbot who received guests had always to find stabling, a difficult task when the riders were expensively mounted gentry or even the king.

Some of the abbot's home and travelling expenses included the making and repairing of carriages and carts, and the provision of leather and webbing for mending the harness, cart cloutes (covers made from canvas) and carriage hoods. Some monks spent their entire lives keeping leather well oiled and polished for which they used a secret preparation. Pack saddles had to be repaired, horses had to be baited and shod, hay, beans and oats had to be gathered in and horse bread had to be baked or purchased, often regardless of expense.

Horses for the monastery were chosen carefully. The master of the horse would be sent to stables to see, try and report on animals before a purchase was agreed. The abbot of Westminster's palfrey – a grey mare whose name is unrecorded – was given special care and had its own groom who gave it 1qt (1 litre) of oil when it was sick and 2lb (900g) of oil of bay to make its coat glossy. The groom also bought a scythe to cut fresh grass for his master's riding horse.

The need for supplies involved the use of pack-horses, which were sent up and down the country to fetch and carry provisions under the supervision of the monastery carters and their boys. As Chaucer and other writers have revealed or surmised, monastic travellers did not have easy journeys. Coachmen rarely knew the way and had no signposts to read. The abbot of Westminster's accounts reveal that when a party was lost, the country people who helped to set it on the right road expected a generous tip for their advice.

Abbots and important dignitaries met frequently, although few reports of their travels and expenses exist. However, the bursar's accounts of Fountains Abbey show that in 1457 the learned Abbot Greenwell often travelled and he recorded every penny that he spent. He went to Middleham Castle to visit the Bishop of Exeter (3s), to the Archbishop of York's house at Bishopthorpe (11s 5d) and journeyed several times to Topcliffe to see the Earl of Northumberland. Abbot Greenwell travelled the not inconsiderable distance to Woburn (£5 6s 8d), to Oxford (£1 17s 9d) and to Meaux (£1 8s 9d).

There was expenditure on a new russet suit for the stable-boy who also received medicine, repairs to his harness, 2lb (900g) of soap, two pairs of gloves and various tips for fetching drink.

The Abbot of Westminster's palfrey – a grey mare whose name is unrecorded – was given special care and had its own groom who gave it 1qt (1 litre) of oil when it was sick and 2lb (900g) of oil of bay to make its coat glossy. The groom also bought a scythe to cut fresh grass for his master's riding horse.

ENTERTAINING

For the purpose of entertaining, the abbot usually had his own kitchen. Although that of Abbot Litlington of Westminster was not a grand place, he did not stint himself or his guests at table. The abbot's favourite dish was fresh salmon and he was determined to have the fish for the great dinner of holy week 1372 that he had planned for his monks. However, his cooks reported that no salmon could be found in the larders of any other monastic houses in London. Undeterred, he sent one of his cooks to Kingston-upon-Thames and then to Hampton, and eventually two fine fresh Thames salmon were obtained for what was then the very large sum of 21s 2d. He also sent six other men on an angling expedition on the Thames to obtain whatever they could catch.

Accounts for great feasts such as that held at the abbot's Islep manor house for the king and his entire household in the same year give a useful indication of what food was available in those days. The gardener would have been called on to supply grapes, apples, pears, cherries, plums and many types of berries from the abbey's gardens, or to procure them for cash or by barter from other gardeners. He would have needed a good supply of onions for garnishing and moderating the taste of strong meat, and herbs for cooking, strewing and for discouraging flies would have been in demand.

The abbot sent men into the West of England to procure wine, although why he could not use his own or buy it locally we can only guess – perhaps it was not good enough. What vintage they obtained is not recorded. However, the abbey treasury yielded up so many precious silver goblets to contain the wine that two horses were needed to carry them and the silver plate. At the same time, an expedition with pack mules and carts went to neighbouring towns to obtain provisions. Apart from foodstuffs, the monks bought linens, towels, napkins to serve the king before dinner, twelve ells of linen that was made into two tablecloths, two 'savenapes' and four ells of 'linen gracie' which one writer suggests was probably used to filter beer.

The spice bill was probably very large, for the cooks required 1lb (454g) of cloves, ½lb (225g) of mace and ¼lb (110g) of ginger; the list also included rice, flour, cinnamon, dates, currants,

ABBOT'S FEAST INCLUDED

Apples, grapes, pears, cherries, plums and assorted berries from the abbey's gardens.

Cloves, mace, ginger, rice, flour, cinnamon, dates, currants, prunes and sugar.

77 capons, 156 pullets, 2 pheasants, 5 heron, 6 egrets and 6 curlew-like birds.

Salt, cream and a large quantity of honey.

prunes and sugar.

An exotic root herb 'galynggale' is mentioned. This was perhaps an aromatic root from the East Indies, of hot bitter taste, to make galantine, which is described as a sauce for any type of roast fowl. Galantine was made from grated bread, beaten cinnamon, ginger, sugar, claret wine and vinegar and was 'as thick as grewelle'.

Also consumed at this banquet were 77 capons, 156 pullets, 2 pheasants, 5 heron, 6 egrets and 6 curlew-like birds. According to the accounts, all the poultry was brought alive from London, probably by the same band of men who had the job of carrying the necessary salt, 6 gal (27 litres) of cream and a large quantity of honey.

The cooks imported 144 tin vessels, 250 wooden bowls which were hired (nine were lost and had to be paid for), five large bowls and four wooden ladles. Five days before the festivity, two men were at work setting up tables, a canvas awning and a screen to hide the buttery from the dining area.

HUNTING ACTIVITIES

Some abbots retained the hunting instincts of their forefathers and went with their retainers to hunt the woods and fish the streams as a way of relaxation and exercise. Stewards would send word of where wild boars, prime fish, deer, game birds and other edible quarry were to be found. Horses, dogs and hawks would be assembled with speed.

Hunting in the fifteenth century was described as necessary for the larder 'with the uncertainty adding excitement to the matter'. There were critics of the activity, as there are now. An abbot of Leicester who liked to spend time with horse and hounds explained that it was his painful duty 'not from delight' but to please the kings and the great lords who were his guests and for the advantage of the house.

The prior of Westacre was accused of spending too much time in the rabbit warren and in rearing swans, which he gave to the local gentry and others free of charge. Canons of Bolton came under fire

for leaving the monastery on bird-watching (possibly wildfowl-netting) expeditions. In 1258 there was a dispute between Hugh, prior of Kirkham, and William de Rhos about the prior's right to hunt with his dogs, 'to wit limers, brachets and hare hounds, and taking all manner of beasts, to wit stags, harts, hinds, foxes and hares'. The prior maintained that his predecessors had hunted the area 'time beyond memory'.

Hawking was growing in popularity among abbots, who practised the art in the monastery gardens. Accounts mention the purchase of meat and chickens to feed the falcons and hawks. Netting was also popular. The monks at Wesminster had large nets slung on the backs of three pack-horses and went in a party with servants to Caversham to stake the nets and prepare traps to catch doves alive. Another hunting party from Westminster departed for Denham; they caught one big boar and Walter the cook who was in the party took a week to cut it up and salt it.

14th century inlaid tiles from Neath Abbey depicting a hunting scene

The Refectory Table

In his Rule, St Benedict had advocated early rising and he made it clear that the meals of the brethren should be scant and frugal.

During the summer months, fruit gathered from the hedges, costard apples, pears and other sorts of soft fruit would brighten up the monks' plain diet. One monk who did not have a good opinion of the variety of food provided in his community complained:

> Yesterday I had peas and pot herbs, today pot herbs and peas; tomorrow I shall eat peas with my pot herbs and the day after pot herbs with my peas.

However, evidence exists that, for some orders at least, food gradually increased both in quality and quantity, and self-denial was not considered necessary. The situation was further improved by pittances, which were special endowments to provide an addition to the monastic fare.

As villages and then towns began to surround important abbeys and temptations increased, it became the custom to serve meals 'plentiful and good' in order to dispel the need for excuses for dining at private houses and inns. The monks could ask for every sort of fish, vegetable, pastry, fruit, cheese and wine, as well as for cider, beer and milk. Spices, figs, ale and cakes were provided annually for Lent. At festivals the monks expected to see the tables laden with pork pies, capons, fig-tarts and blancmange of rice with almonds.

At first, Benedict's Rule was not questioned by the monk-gardeners who were skilful with their bill-hooks, axes and spades. They and their brothers had sufficient challenges in clearing the acres of scrub and heath and cutting wood for fires and timber to build their huts and small church. They planned gardens of the future and made small plots between the boulders in which they grew beans and other green vegetables.

POTTAGE

This is a modern version of a recipe that was used by a cook in a monastery kitchen. Note that the thickening is made with breadcrumbs – the potato was unknown in England at this time.

INGREDIENTS

1lb (500g) shelled peas
8oz (200g) chopped cabbage
2pt (1 litre) stock or water
Handful of parsley
2 sprigs of hyssop
4oz (100g) soft breadcrumbs
salt and pepper to taste

METHOD

Cook the peas and cabbage in the stock or water for 30 minutes until tender. Chop the parsley and hyssop finely and add to the liquid, stirring well. Press the mixture through a sieve or blend in a liquidiser. Mix the breadcrumbs, salt and pepper and reheat slowly. Serve piping hot with a small loaf of bread the size of a round scone.

SAUCE VERT

INGREDIENTS

2tbsp (30ml) fresh chopped mint
1tbsp (15ml) fresh chopped parsley
1tbsp (15ml) fresh chopped hyssop
1 garlic clove, crushed
1 cupful of cider vinegar
2oz (50g) soft breadcrumbs
salt and pepper

METHOD

Mix the herbs together with the garlic and add the breadcrumbs and cider vinegar. Add the salt and pepper and leave to absorb the different flavours. If the sauce is too thick, add more cider vinegar to give a pouring consistency.

Even when it was realised that few men could survive on the monastic diet and their rations were increased, the winter meal and the main meal of summer were still extremely frugal. Apart from feast days, when meals would be supplemented by, for example, extra fruit, a meal generally consisted of little more than pottage – a thick vegetable soup. In addition, there would be a portion of bread and a mug of ale. Occasionally, fresh or salted fish accompanied by a green herb salad dressed with vinegar and oil would be served.

For many years Benedictine monks kept strictly to their rule of life which forbade the eating of flesh meat, although they did provide it for visitors, the sick and certain estate workers. Meat was understood to mean flesh of any sort, including birds and fish, and the rule was strictly enforced by most abbots and other heads of houses. Later, however, flesh meat was interpreted as the flesh of four-footed beasts.

By the twelfth century, the rule regarding the monks' vegetarian diet was relaxed as it was considered too difficult to follow in the wet, windy and generally cold climate of England, which did not have the food-growing advantages of more favourable climes.

The rule regarding the times and amount of meals was also relaxed, but the monks were required to observe strict order and ceremony 'in accordance with the manner and customs of polite folk' at all meal-times. The monks had to wash their hands at a special place in the cloister, enter the frater (dining hall) in silence and each bow to the high table. According to ceremony, they had to stand in their own places until the abbot or prior walked to his seat and rang a small bell. At that signal, the priest on duty for that week would say grace, to which all the monks responded. The brothers would then be seated and, when a monk who stood in a pulpit on the west wall began to read, the servants entered from the kitchens with the food.

Detailed instructions were laid down that the servers should work quickly and quietly and they were not to disturb the diners. The monks themselves were instructed to be quiet while eating. On the rare and special occasions when nuts were served, they were to be opened quietly with a knife and not cracked open between the teeth.

No man was to leave the room or to walk about. Salt had to be taken with the point of the knife, not with the fingers. When a man drank, he was required to hold the cup with both hands. He was not permitted to wipe either his knife or his fingers on the table-cloth, nor to put his fingers into his cup.

When the meal was over, the abbot or prior would ring the bell once more and the brethren would walk out in file to the church, at the same time singing the 51st psalm in thanks for their repast. If the meal was in the afternoon before dark, the monks would rest for an hour in the dorter. Then they would rise, wash and go to church for nones. After supper, the monks would assemble in the cloister when one of the choir monks would read to his fellows from either the Bible or another holy book. The brothers would then return to the church, sing compline and retire for the night.

Apart from bread and ale, pottage formed the staple diet of the monks during the Middle Ages. Pottage was also known as 'porray' and 'sewe' and was a thick vegetable soup. It was the monk-gardener's duty to provide the necessary vegetables to fill two of the three cauldrons of boiling water that stood ready each day in the abbey kitchens. Similar supplies went to the kitchens of the abbot and the guest-house master, if these departments were large enough to have kitchens of their own.

One of the cauldrons was filled with broad beans, which the gardener grew in large quantities. In the other, various vegetables were cooked, the favourite being the leaves of colewort, leeks, onions, garlic and peas; parsley and chives were added to provide flavour.

The gardener would also have supplied salad crops such as alexanders, lettuce, radish, cress, water-cress, groundsel, borage, wild celery, catnip, tansy, chervil, sweet cicely and a type of spinach. Some of these vegetables and herbs would have been added to the second cauldron, while others would have been eaten raw as a relish.

Four large dishes were kept beside the cauldrons: one dish was for the beans, which were removed from the cauldron when half-cooked; another, much larger and standing in running water, was for washing the vegetables; the third was for washing up and the fourth contained hot water for the weekly washing of feet and the shaving of monks' faces and tonsures. Large spoons were kept separate for stirring the beans, the vegetables and for seasoning the pottage.

So that the monks' habits might remain clean and to prevent the cooks from burning themselves, the refector (the monk in charge) provided four pairs of sleeves for the servers, gloves for moving the dishes of hot vegetables in the kitchen and towels (changed once a week) for wiping the serving dishes. Knife-sharpening stones, strainers, urns, ladles, bellows, utensils for feeding the fire and stands for the pots had their proper places.

The monks were instructed to be quiet while eating. On the rare and special occasions when nuts were served, they were to be opened quietly with a knife and not cracked open between the teeth.

No man was to leave the room or to walk about. Salt had to be taken with the point of the knife, not with the fingers. When a man drank, he was required to hold the cup with both hands. He was not permitted to wipe either his knife or his fingers on the table-cloth, nor to put his fingers into his cup.

Leek

Four cooks were appointed from among the brethren each week. When the vesper bell sounded, their orders were to pray and then to collect the ration of beans that had been freshly picked by the monk-gardener and his assistant that morning. The cooks would wash the vegetables before soaking them in cold water in the cauldron.

The next day, after lauds, the cooks would wash themselves and set the cauldron to boil. As the skins of the beans loosened, the monks would remove them from the cauldron and set them aside for compost. The cauldron of washing-up water was then heated on the fire, and as the water began to bubble the four cooks said the divine office together. The cauldron of vegetables, which had been placed on the fire after the gospel of the morning mass, was then prepared.

In the Middle Ages, cooking vessels were either iron stewpots or cauldrons. At table, meals would have been eaten with a single knife, a piece of board or a slice of stale bread serving as a plate. The bread was called a trencher, so a person who ate both his food and his bread was called a 'good trencherman'.

Pottage or soup was served in wooden bowls, from which the food was supped. Until the invention of forks, the diner would use his knife to cut the food into pieces and then would pick it up with his fingers. Nuts and fruit were usually served after a meal.

LEEKS FOR LENT

The seasoning of food during Lent and at other times of the year – ie, meat days and non-meat days – has always been of interest to cooks. In *The Herbal Review* (Vol 3, No 41) Colin S. Dence quotes from the detailed account of a merchant in 1393:

> There be three sorts of porray, according to the saying of cooks, who call them white, green and black. White porray is so called because it is made of the white of the leek, chines, chitterlings and ham, in the autumn and winter seasons on meat days; and know that no other fat than pig's fat is good therewith. And first you pick over wash slice and blanch the leeks, to wit in summer when they be young; but in winter when the leeks be older and harder, it behoves you to parboil them, instead of blanching them, and if it be a fish day, after what has been said, you must put them in a pot of hot water and boil them, and also boil sliced onions and fry the onions, and afterwards fry the leeks with the onions; then put all to cook in a pot of cow's milk, if it be out of Lent and on a fish day; and if it be in Lent one puts Milk of Almonds therein.

As Mr Dence points out, on a meat day, porray was a meat-based dish, on a fish day cow's milk replaced the ham, but during Lent almond milk was used as a substitute. The almond milk, which provided the necessary protein, was made by crushing the nuts in a mortar and soaking them in water overnight.

FISH AND FOWL

As a source of food, fish was very important to the monastic community. The carp, tench, roach, perch, bream, eels and pike which were fattened in the abbey's fish-pond were a welcome change from the salted fish which was frequently served at table. Fish was also important when meat was not permitted during fast days or when flesh was scarce and expensive.

Splendid drawings of fish such as carp, trout and eels often feature in early illustrations of monks at table. At Castle Acre near the east coast, large quantities of oyster shells were discovered when the site was excavated. This has raised the question whether the oysters were eaten as a luxury food or whether they were commonplace in the Middle Ages.

Carp was both popular and plentiful. It has been estimated that an acre of water stocked with this fish produced more food than an acre of land sown with wheat – and with considerably less trouble and expense.

Fish-ponds were also an attraction to duck, geese and water-fowl – another source of food that provided a welcome addition to the monastic diet on feast days and other special occasions. The damp areas around the ponds yielded plentiful supplies of rushes and sweet-smelling herbs for strewing over the monastery floors. Willows provided wood for fencing.

It was not unusual for an abbey to have as many as three ponds. One would be stocked with pike, another with less predatory fish and a third, called the stew pond, with fish ready to be taken out for consumption. Stew ponds were normally divided into sections to keep different types of fish from eating each other and to make catching them less difficult. The first two ponds would have been fished in sequence, leaving time between each piscatorial harvest for the smaller fish to mature.

Good examples of stew ponds may be seen at Michelham Priory, Newstead Abbey and Ely. Abbots often had their ponds stocked with their favourite fish and as a means of relaxation, some abbots would fish for their suppers themselves.

When fish was to be served at meal-time, one of the abbey servants would be instructed to go down to the pond and 'net a fine fat fish'.

At many religious houses, fresh fish were obtained as dues. Ely is thought to have gained its name because tithes were paid to the abbey in eels. A surprisingly large number of fish were consumed by the community at Ely. A total of twenty-three thousand eels were provided each year by a neighbouring parish, yet only seventy monks were in residence.

Apart from eels, the variety of fresh fish caught and eaten in monastic times was considerable and most communities made special provision for dealing with them. Excavations at a Templar establishment at Washford, near Redditch, have revealed a fish house and a curing furnace associated with nearby ponds and breeding tanks. The abbots of Glastonbury's stone-built fish house at Meare, Somerset, still survives.

According to Prior Moore's record of expenditure on the fish-ponds of the Worcester manors, he stocked his tanks at regular intervals with eel, perch, roach, tench and pickerel.

The brethren of Chester had a free boat on the River Dee, plus fishing rights off Anglesey for a ship and ten nets and the tithes of some of the best fisheries in the country. All rivers had to keep the

Monks loved a good story, and one often told on fish days was about the marvellous whale which, one day, they hoped to see. According to legend, the great fish loved to rest on the top of the sea for as long as it took for grass to grow on its back. Mariners would then be tempted to land there, thinking they had found a new island, but as soon as their cooking stove was alight the whale would slowly submerge and consume the sailors for his supper.

The drawing is taken from Queen Mary's Psalter, a form of natural-history book very popular in the Middle Ages.

centre of the stream clear of nets; at Chester it was to be wide enough for a boat 25ft (7.6m) broad with oars 16ft (5m) long. Monks at Vale Royal let their weirs at Watford for an annual rent of 48 'strikes' of eels and twelve large eels annually.

Fresh fish was sufficiently important for monasteries to acquire exclusive rights to fish rivers and other waters. They also considered those rights valuable enough to fight for them in court or, as happened in one extraordinary case, to resort to hiring fighters on their behalf.

In a dispute over the rights to fish over Hornsea and Wassand mere, the contestants – the abbots of rival monastic houses – indulged in the practice of a 'judicial duel'. According to a chronicler, they appointed hired fighters (their champions) at York who fought violently until the justices brought the dispute to an end.

In 1342, the abbot of Byland sued fourteen men 'who by force of arms did break the banks of the river Derwent at Rillington by which the water issued from the breaches and so flooded the abbot's pasture that there was a loss of ten pounds'.

However, it was not only the abbot who valued fishing rights. Others of the non-religious community were apparently prepared to commit murder to maintain their right to take fresh fish. One of many disputes recorded concerns Hugh Venables of Kinderton Hall who, having fallen foul of the abbot of Vale Royal in 1426 concerning fishing rights, took his revenge by plundering one of the granges and driving off the cattle.

Furthermore, on Shrove Tuesday, 'not dreading God', Venables maimed the abbot's bailiff and left him for dead. During Easter week, Venables damaged the abbot's mill and hacked the machinery to pieces. Then, with his retainers, he laid in wait day and night with the intention of maiming the monks and their servants and of slaying the abbot. According to the record, the man so frightened the monks that they dared not minister to the abbey 'during this time of dread'.

So incensed was Venables regarding his fishing rights that he even ignored letters from the king who eventually ordered the justices of Chester to punish the man and keep him in prison 'for the great riots, exorcions and oppressions and the horrible and cruel murders he has done to the officers, tenants and servants of the said monastery'.

In 1239 there occurred the curious case of the abbot of Byland who sued Peter de Brus for eight thousand haddocks. Apparently, de Brus had agreed to pay the abbot one thousand haddocks in rent and was well in arrears.

Fish was cooked simply and was often flavoured with herbs, saffron and other spices; if it seemed a little rancid, the flavour was masked with vinegar and verjuice. The whole fish was placed in a cauldron which was filled with water and sometimes ale and the pot was hung over a wide fireplace. For baking, there were flat pans, similar to a frying pan, with a long handle. A grid made of metal bars, also with a long handle, acted as an elementary form of grill.

Since monastic recipes are hard to decipher and do not specify quantities and cooking times, it is necessary to compromise. The directions which follow are based on what the monks ate and, hopefully, will inspire those interested in monastic food to conduct their own culinary experiments.

> Lord. Let me catch a fish
> So Large that even I,
> In telling of it afterwards,
> Shall have no need to lie.

The following fish were eaten by monks during the Middle Ages:

Fresh-water fish: carp, eels, salmon, chub, grayling, trout and crayfish.

Shellfish: crabs, mussels, shrimps, lobsters and oysters.

Sea-water fish: cod, herrings, skate, haddock, plaice and sole.

Salted Fish

Salted fish was eaten frequently by medieval monks, particularly during Lent. Great care had to be taken in preparing the fish for the table, as preservation methods were primitive and the fish skin would be hard and stiff. According to one scribe, the taste and condition of salted fish were reasons

ABBOTS FIGHT DUEL

In a dispute over the rights to fish over Hornsea and Wassand mere, the contestants – the abbots of rival monastic houses – indulged in the practice of a 'judicial duel'. According to a chronicler, they appointed hired fighters (their champions) at York who fought violently until the justice brought the dispute to an end.

why many condiments such as ground pepper and mustard were required.

John Russell, in his *Book of Nurture*, says stockfish could be coaxed back to some measure of softness using 'many waters of times renewed'. It was also necessary to be firm, for 'the white hering by the bak abroad ye spate him sure'. When roe and bones were out, 'then may your lord endure to eat merrily with mustard'.

A delicacy enjoyed by Russell was baked herring dressed and dished with white sugar. He most enjoyed the belly of pike and was also fond of lamprey which, if salted, had to be cut into seven 'gobbets' and eaten with onions and galantine.

Little was wasted in the monastery kitchen. The dripping from herrings was sent to the cobbler's shop at Beaulieu for softening leather.

Prices of fresh fish and fish ready salted were high. The demand was in many cases greater than the supply, as sea angling was an unmechanised and hazardous occupation, with poor and inadequate tackle and boats. The carriage, especially of salt-water fish, was also a costly item. Until the fifteenth century, sea fishing was carried out almost entirely from the south-east of England. Only after the fifteenth century were the sailors from Bristol, with the aid of the mariner's compass, able to reach and take their share of the northern fisheries.

RECIPES

The sweet/sour flavour that was so popular in medieval dishes can be achieved by cooking fish with parsnips.

Sweet-Sour Fish

INGREDIENTS
4 cod steaks, approx 1in (2.5cm) thick
1 onion
1lb (400g) parsnips
1tbsp (1×15ml) oatmeal
1tsp (1×5ml) chopped parsley
1tsp (1×5ml) chopped marjoram
pinch of saffron
salt and pepper

METHOD
Rub the cod steaks with a little raw onion and salt. Sprinkle a little pepper over, dust with oatmeal, then fry until golden brown. Arrange the fish pieces on a greased fireproof dish. Chop the onion and parsnips finely and fry together until golden brown. Put the vegetables around the fish and fill any cracks with chopped parsley, marjoram and the saffron. Cover with tinfoil and bake in a slow oven, Gas Mark 2, 300°F (150°C) for ¾ of an hour. Serve in the dish in which it is cooked. The parsnips add the important sweet element and saffron adds a delicate aroma and fine golden tint.

Monastery Mackerel

Small fresh mackerel are grilled quickly and served with a green salad. Large mackerel are better baked and stuffed and are equally delicious.

INGREDIENTS
4 whole mackerel, about 8oz (200g) each
1 crumbled bay leaf

For the stuffing
4oz (100g) fine breadcrumbs
2oz (50g) butter
1 onion, finely chopped
1tbsf (1×15ml) chopped parsley
1tsp (1×5ml) chopped marjoram
2oz (50g) butter
salt and pepper

METHOD
Slit the mackerel and open flat to remove the spine (it should come away easily). Mix together the stuffing ingredients and fill between the two sides of the mackerel. Place on a greased fireproof dish and sprinkle the crumbled bay leaf over the top. Add small knobs of butter, then bake in a medium oven, Gas Mark 4, 350°F (180°C) for 30 minutes. Eat immediately with a green salad or boiled broad beans.

The Abbot's Salmon

INGREDIENTS
1 salmon weighing 4lb (2kg)
1tbsf (1×15ml) salt
1tbsf (1×15ml) coriander seeds
1tbsf (1×15ml) vinegar
1tbsf (1×15ml) cooking oil
1 crumbled bay leaf

METHOD
Make a few shallow cuts on one side of the fish. Mix together the salt, coriander seed and oil. Sprinkle half this mixture inside the fish and the rest over the cuts. Place the fish on tinfoil paper and pour over the vinegar, bay leaf and cooking oil. Wrap up tightly and place on a baking tray. Cook for 30 minutes at Gas Mark 5, 375°F (190°C). Serve either hot or leave to cool in the tinfoil paper. There should be well-flavoured juices to serve with the fish. If served cold, these will set into a jelly.

Jellied Eels

INGREDIENTS
2 eels, approx 8oz (200g) each
1 onion, chopped
2 bay leaves
2 sprigs thyme
2 sprigs parsley
2 cupfuls cider
pinch of saffron

METHOD
Chop the eel into pieces approx 1in (2.5cm) thick and place in a shallow earthenware dish. Between the spaces put the chopped onion, bay leaves, thyme, parsley and saffron. Pour over the cider and cover. Bake in a slow oven, Gas Mark 2, 300°F (150°C) for approx 2 hours or until the eel pieces are tender. Remove the herbs and leave overnight. Next day, the majority of the bones will have dissolved and the eel can be served with brown bread and butter and a green salad.

Sauces for Fish

The following two recipes, which were the type of sauces enjoyed by medieval monks, fit in well with today's ideas for flavouring fish.

Green Butter

INGREDIENTS
1 handful of fresh parsley
1 cupful boiling water
1 small onion
4oz (100g) butter
salt and pepper

METHOD
Pour the boiling water over the parsley and leave to soak for ½ hour. Pour through a sieve and keep the soaked parsley. Either chop this or blend in the liquidiser. Blend the onion to a pulp in the liquidiser or chop finely. Mix this with the parsley, salt and pepper and add the butter which should be just warm but not melted. Chill in the refrigerator until needed.

Fennel Sauce

INGREDIENTS
2tbsf (1×15ml) chopped fennel leaves
4oz (100g) butter

METHOD
Melt the butter in a heavy-based pan over a low heat and add the finely chopped fennel leaves. Cook for 2 minutes and pour over the fish.

PIGEONS IN THE COTE

Dovecotes filled with fat pigeons were another source of fresh food for the religious community in winter. Pigeons cost little to feed for there was plenty of food for them in the land that surrounded the abbey. The birds belonged to the abbot or prior for, as lord of the manor, only he would have enjoyed the privilege and right to maintain a pigeon house, or dovecote as it was known. He was allowed only one dovecote, but its size was not restricted. Some dovecotes were very large, housing between one and two thousand birds which were all free to leave by day and return in the evening.

These tall and often elaborate structures, which were first used by the Romans, were employed extensively in the early Middle Ages. Before root crops were introduced to feed cattle during winter, it was the custom to slaughter all but a few of the livestock required for breeding and to salt this down for the kitchen. It was a wasteful exercise; what was killed could not breed the following year and carcases often rotted through the use of unskilled salting. Pigeons from the dovecotes, hares from the pastures, rabbits from the warrens and fish from the stewponds were a welcome change in the monks' diet. And in spring and summer, pigeon pies and pigeon eggs would also have been enjoyed.

Initially, it was difficult to persuade the pigeons to return to the dovecote but this problem was overcome by providing safe and easily accessible nesting and breeding places. The birds would be enticed with a few handfuls of grain and peas until they became used to the house.

In the mid-seventeenth century, about twenty-six thousand dovecotes were standing, but few remain now. Some were tall, tower-like structures, others were timber-framed like houses; a few formed parts of barns and houses, and a number were circular with a tiled roof, a lantern and a dormer window.

GAME

Venison abounded in many abbey parks and would have formed part of the abbot's diet, if not that of the more humble monks. Swans, otters, water voles and squirrels were also eaten, as were birds such as blackcock, heron, partridge, pheasant, quail, snipe, teal, woodcock and the ever present plover (lap-wing) and sea-gull. Small birds such as blackbirds, thrushes, sparrows and even owls were placed into many a monastic cooking-pot and would have been enjoyed with a bowl of ale or cider. Even birds of prey such as the merlin fell frequently to the monastic arrow or net.

As winter approached, the obedientiaries who were responsible for catering for the community began to make plans for stocking the larders. St Martin's day, 11 November, was the usual date for deciding the number of livestock that could be maintained bearing in mind the available hay. What could not be fed until spring was destined for the salting tubs. This was the time when the old and unsaleable animals from the herds or those no longer suitable for the yoke would be culled. Analysis of bones found in different parts of the country have shown no regular pattern for slaughtering animals except in the sheep-breeding areas. Sheep were bred primarily for their wool, so mutton was not popularly eaten.

The gardener would also have been busy gathering those seeds and roots he wanted to keep free from frost for planting the following year. He would also have made his final harvest of onions, a vegetable constantly in demand when strong salted meat was served so frequently and garnishing vegetables were few.

PROVISIONS FROM TOWNS AND FAIRS

Provisions which could not be obtained from their own gardens or estates, the brethren purchased at local market towns and fairs. The provisioners, often advised by the gardener or led by him in his own horse and cart as part of a slow-moving column, made their way along the pot-holed dirt-tracks to nearby towns, often as regularly as once a week. If the necessary goods such as spices and fine wines could not be obtained locally, the provisioners journeyed to London or another large city or port.

The monks from the monasteries at Battle and Glastonbury frequently went to London to obtain better quality salted fish, even making their way there in mid winter when travelling was difficult. The carters, freed from their farm work, had little else to do in winter.

The monks of Ely had their own boat for the

AS WINTER APPROACHED

The gardener would also have been busy gathering those seeds and roots he wanted to keep free from frost for planting the following year. He would also have made his final harvest of onions, a vegetable constantly in demand when strong salted meat was served so frequently and garnishing vegetables were few.

purpose of carrying grain from Cambridge to their abbey. Those who sailed – men under obligation to the abbot – received five black loaves and five draughts of common ale from the granator, plus nine eggs or nine herrings from the cellarer. If they arrived on a day when it was permitted to eat meat, the sailors would be given two dishes of meat.

The monks of Beaulieu were not only boat owners but fish processors, too. So great was their need for fish in the winter that they set up their own fish-drying facilities near the East Anglian port of Great Yarmouth for the drying and 'kippering' of herrings.

The men of Battle often bought their meat at the market set up near the abbey gates and their less expensive wine from Winchelsea. Other provisions which were not available locally came from Sandwich and Canterbury, or from Faversham when there were markets and fairs.

Fresh sea fish was in considerable demand and among the fish bought direct from the fishermen were barbel, cod, conger eels, gunard, hake, herring, lamprey, ling, plaice, porpoise, ray, sole, sprats, smelts, shrimps, whiting and shellfish, including cockles, mussels and oysters.

An analysis of an abbot's household accounts from Michaelmas 1371 to 1373 shows that more than thirty kinds of fish were bought in the two-year period. The list includes green fish; hard fish, also known as stock-fish and so heavily salted; and smaller fish such as haddock and herrings, which was salted and preserved in barrels. Other fish for the larder were salted salmon, red herring and salted eels.

Barns were of considerable advantage to communities in need of dry and secure storage space for winter supplies. Many barns held provisions that had been acquired from local tithes and rents, but the abbey's granges also helped to fill them with grain and foodstuffs for the refectory and guest-house, and also for the oxen and horses which were essential to abbey life. Some barns would have combined storage with the keeping of pigeons and small domestic animals such as pigs and goats. Fire and theft appear to have been the two major hazards.

Fruits of the Vine
and
Orchard

One of the ambitions of a monk-gardener with a reputation to uphold was to grow grapes that would be regarded as of sufficient quality to make wine for the community and even for communion. The grapes grown in English monastery gardens were rarely sweet enough to be served at the abbot's table, but they were given to sick monks in the infirmary and to make various medical beverages. Unlike French grapes, the English variety was neither big nor juicy. However, the monks were pleased if they achieved a crop of fruit and there was always the chance that they could persuade those travelling abroad to bring back roots and cuttings of varieties more suitable for a northern climate.

One particular problem with vines was that as they grew, they became covered with a sticky, oozing substance, on which transparent green-winged flies fed avidly. Fearing for the vigour of the plants, one monk-gardener sought the advice of an 'expert' who was staying overnight in the guest-house. He duly poured over the vine an infusion of soapwort root, southernwood leaves and chopped onions. The sticky substance, he observed, responded by growing even more profusely.

Like most good gardeners at that time, the monk knew that the reason his grapes would never make great wines was not his lack of skill, but the English climate. As far back as AD 79, the Roman Emperor Tacitus had written of Britain that 'the climate is wretched with its frequent rains and mists' and that the soil produced good crops 'except olives and vines'.

Waterworks at Canterbury

A period called the 'Little Optimum' that occurred during the eleventh and twelfth centuries had been a harrowing time for monastic gardeners. This period had been followed by droughts, floods and tempests through much of the following two centuries. And in the first half of the fifteenth century, many vineyards and orchards throughout the country were destroyed by severe frost.

In earlier years, vine-growing in Britain was by all accounts a profitable, although time-consuming business. An early picture of an English monastery garden with its vineyard and orchard is derived from a rough and simple plan of Canterbury's waterworks and drainage system. This was drawn in 1165, five years before the murderers of Thomas à Becket assembled under a mulberry tree in an adjoining orchard before carrying out their historic deed.

In his life of St Aldhelm, William of Malmesbury says that vines were originally planted on a hill to the north of the abbey, perhaps on the slope on the far side of Newntom Water. They were set there in about 1030 by a Greek monk called Constantine, who took refuge in the house for several years. Constantine was certainly a gardener and could well have been a person of some importance, for an historian wrote that he attired himself in a pall before his death and the whiteness and smell of his bones was 'significant' when his grave was later disturbed.

The planting of vineyards was a popular pursuit after 1066 when William the Conqueror's reign brought stability to the country. Glastonbury Abbey had several centuries earlier received the gift of a vineyard from King Alfred's grandson, King Edward. Now other abbeys took up cultivation of the vine. One of these was Battle, near the place where Harold's men met their fate in 1066.

It seems unlikely that the monks of Malmesbury, Battle and other religious houses enjoyed the produce of the English vine. Wine making was not a popular activity and English wine was drunk only when supplies from the continent were not available. In all probability, English monks preferred a well-brewed beer, even though it was brewed from oats, to a wine made from sour grapes.

Later, better rootstock was introduced and the weather

improved. The figure of 45 vineyards in 15 counties that was recorded in the 1080s had increased to 139 by the time of Henry VIII, and of these 52 were cultivated by the religious communities. Furthermore, not all of the wine was reserved for the holy communion table.

The quantities of wine, cider and beer that were consumed by the religious and lay brothers in the monasteries and granges appears to have been prodigious. For example, the canons of St Paul's each had an allowance of 30gal (136 litres) of beer per week, and those of Waltham six bottles per week, each sufficient for ten men at a single meal. However, it should be noted that tea and coffee were unknown and pond water was to be feared. Furthermore, the absence of fresh vegetables and thirst-quenching fruit for most of the year may have been another factor in the quantity of alcohol that was drunk.

THE DRINK THAT CHEERS

One of the guidelines laid down by St Benedict in his rule for monastic life was that each monk should be allocated a measure of wine each day. This proposition posed no problem for the monks in France and Italy, where vineyards were cultivated extensively in the warm climate, but it was impossible to observe in Britain because of the cold climate. It was agreed, therefore, that when no wine was available locally, the monks should accept the situation and be served beer or some other suitable drink instead.

St Benedict was diffident in stating the exact quantity of any sort of beverage that the brothers should drink. However, he was careful to point out that they should not drink their fill, but they should sup sparingly, since too much 'led even wise men into infidelity'. He commended those 'to whom God had granted the capacity to abstain'. Although this was good advice which the brethren took seriously, during the long, hard winter months, warming drinks would generally be considered essential.

APPLES FOR CIDER

Religious communities that were founded before the Norman Conquest had made good use of the common

crab apple, taking it from the wild and crushing it, to make an acidic unfermented liquid called verjuice. The small bitter-tasting apples brought in by the French after 1066, however, were infinitely better.

The common practice was to plant ungrafted seedlings of crab or other cider apples in the hedges and open fields. There they were left to grow on until they bore sufficient fruit for the cider maker to judge whether they were good enough to leave ungrafted. This resulted in a large variety of cider apples and a considerable variation in the quality of the drink.

The monk-gardener was generally responsible for supervising production of cider. Sometimes this took place in the orchard soon after the apples had been gathered, but usually there was a special cider-making area within the monastery compound. During the twelfth century, the gardener at Glastonbury had his own cider house, a small building in the south-west of the ground which can still be seen. It was from one of his orchards, replanted by Showerings in 1974, that he was able to report that he had made 31 tuns of cider at the rate of one tun to every eight quarters of apples pressed.

The gardener distributed 20 tuns to the cellarer and the same amount for the men who were hayricking. Two tuns were sent to the abbot's house at Mells. The pittancer, an obedientiary who served it to the brethren on special days, received a single tun. The gardener sold 3 tuns, the income benefiting his gardening expenses.

The Glastonbury gardener also harvested 3 bushels of pears from the abbey orchard. He sent a bushel to the abbot and the rest to be enjoyed by the monks.

The monks usually made cider at the end of the horticultural year when there was little else to do and the weather was too wet to go out on the land. The apples, probably called 'cider sorts' or 'bittersweets', as they still are today, would have been allowed to fall or helped to the ground with long ash sticks called 'panking poles'. Other long sticks, called 'hook poles', were used for giving the branches a vigorous shake. Unless there was an immediate need for them, the apples were left in heaps where they fell or piled up in tumps between the trees. The apples were regarded as 'mellow' and ready to use when the cider maker could push his thumb easily into the flesh. (Mellowing is rarely practised nowadays as it is thought that apples left too long on the ground tend to lose sugar.)

The method of extracting the juice is first to crush the fruit and then to press the pulp. In monastic times and for hundreds of years afterwards, juice was taken from the apples by crushing them in a dolly tub, which was not unlike a large pestle and mortar. The pulp was then poured into a trough – usually one of the long halves of a hollowed-out log – and rolled several times with a heavy circular millstone. The trough had a hole to allow the juice to escape into a wooden bucket or other container. If large quantities of cider were made, the monks would construct more permanent extraction and pressing equipment that needed the pulling power of a horse or donkey.

Cider was fermented without the addition of yeast and stored in wooden casks. The method of fermentation prevented the build-up of dioxide and resulted in a still cider of great character. 'Scrumpy' is available today on farmsteads and from the occasional country pub in cider-making districts. Perry was made from pears using the same methods as for cider-making.

HOME-BREWED ALE

Private ale-making as opposed to brewing for the community was a simple matter that required nothing but bog myrtle, malt, sugar, dried yeast and fresh clean water. Sampling the brew after it had fermented for a week and then stood for a week was always an enjoyable and heart-warming occasion.

The traditional brewers' herbs were mugwort and ale-cost, the ripe berries of the common elder and dandelions that had been gathered from the cloister garth and around the monastery wall. Other useful herbs for ale-making were heather and nettles.

Yarrow, a herb which often grew better as a weed in the lawns than in the infirmarer's garden, was almost as much in demand as bog myrtle and produced an excellent beer. One infirmarian used the herb to stop bleeding and to make 'milfoil' tea to dispel melancholy. However, when

---

CIDER

Cider was fermented without the addition of yeast and stored in wooden casks. The method of fermentation prevented the build-up of dioxide and resulted in a still cider of great character. 'Scrumpy' is available today on farmsteads and from the occasional country pub in cider-making districts. Perry was made from pears using the same methods as for cider-making but in smaller quantities.

Brewer's Herbs

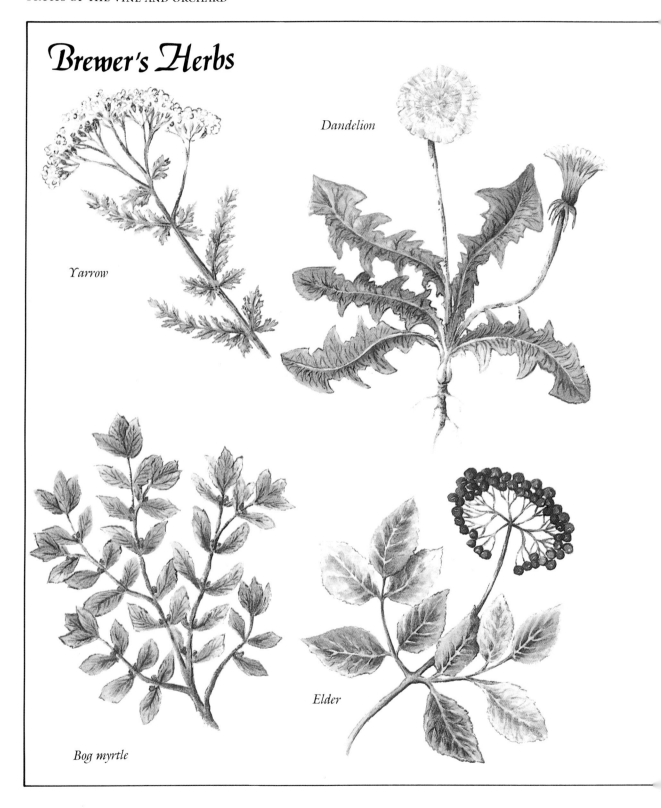

Yarrow

Dandelion

Bog myrtle

Elder

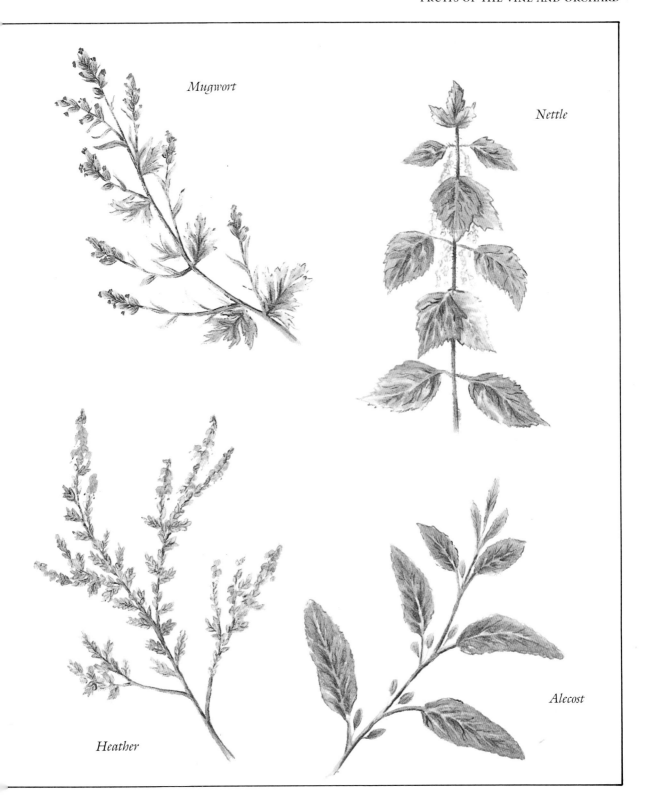

Mugwort

Nettle

Heather

Alecost

he realised that yarrow beer was beneficial for lifting the spirit, he began to prescribe it for medicinal purposes.

Where only natural ingredients were available, such as at distant granges or at times when the abbey stores were firmly locked, it was customary to brew a potent beer from the leaves of meadow sweet, betony and agrimony, with the addition of quantities of the herb angelica to supply the sweetness. When sugar was available, this replaced angelica.

The monks also made ales and beer from fermented grain, as did the monastery brewer. They looked to monk-gardener Stephen and his gardens for the plants that would give the beer a good flavour, excellent body and a longer life in the cask. Mugwort was useful in this respect as was yarrow, betony and ground ivy – which was added for the bitter taste.

In an age of superstition, the monks would tie iris roots together and hang them from the edge of the barrels to prevent the brew from turning sour. If this remedy failed and the beer spoilt, the monks would 'take lupins, lay them on the four quarters of the dwelling and over the door, and under the thresh-hold, and under the ale vat', and then put the plants into the ale with holy water. The source of the holy water has not been stated, but obedientiaries who were anxious to please the brewers would no doubt have been helpful.

The infirmarer took a special interest in the private ale-making for he needed the brew as medicine for those in his care. A monk who was unwell and who needed purging was more likely to take his medicine when it was a mug of ale, irrespective of the fact that wormwood and senna had been added.

Those with scurvy, a common complaint, consumed an ale which included the juice of scurvy grass, sage and cresses. A popular drink to give a low-spirited monk fresh vitality was a regular mug of ale that had been thickened with eggs, butter, sugar and selected spices.

HERBAL WINES

The gardens and grounds that adjoined the abbey also yielded adequate quantities of plants from which the monks made wine. One of the several beverages that had a reputation for clearing the palate, aiding the digestion and expelling flatulence was wormwood. This bitter herb – which was used mainly to deter fleas – was steeped in wine in portions of a handful to a gallon. The method was probably passed on to monks who visited Rome. The wine, which was highly prized in Roman times, was used to toast victors of chariot races.

A more sophisticated appetiser was a cordial wine called Hippocras. It was made by infusing a mixture of spices in red and white wine that was sweetened with sugar and honey.

Agrimony, the sweet-smelling plant that was often used by the infirmarian as an effective gargle for those monks who had lost their voices, was in plentiful supply. The monks used large bunches of the herb to make a wine to help their brothers who were suffering from insomnia. The herb was also infused as a tea for the relief of skin and liver disorders, a common problem in winter when the daily diet consisted mainly of salted fish from the store and was lacking in fresh fruit.

Wine which was made from balm leaves together with raisins, sugar, an orange, a lemon and yeast, was considered a remedy for fevers and colds. Easier to make and with fewer ingredients were wines made from borage, blackberries, broom, clover, dandelion, elder, cowslip and woodbine (honeysuckle).

ORCHARDS AND FRUIT GARDENS

Orchards and fruit gardens have long been associated with monastic life and it is difficult to believe that a few centuries after the Norman Conquest many in Britain were so neglected that thousands of once-loved and bountiful trees stood neglected and dying. Enthusiasm declined not because of lack of desire by the monks to eat fruit but because the Black Death had carried off many of their willing workers.

The long period of bitter winters and cold summers were also to blame, but, according to the Dean of Windsor, there were other reasons for the decline in orchards. He pointed an accusing finger at the idleness of those

---

AGRIMONY

Agrimony, the sweet-smelling plant that was often used by the infirmarian as an effective gargle for those monks who had lost their voices, was in plentiful supply. The monks used large bunches of the herb to make a wine to help their brothers who were suffering from insomnia. The herb was also infused as a tea for the relief of skin and liver disorders, a common problem in winter when the daily diet consisted mainly of salted fish from the store and was lacking in fresh fruit.

who had grown rich, those who were no longer frugal and those who imported from other countries that which they could have grown themselves.

Gradually, however, as the epidemic faded and more young men who were keen on gardening entered the monasteries, there began a revival of interest in the planting of orchards. Even the dean was forced to declare that such fruits as delicate apples, 'plummes', 'peares', walnut and 'filberds' were to be found. He also noted that such 'strange fruits' as apricots, almonds, peaches and 'figges' could be found in noblemen's (and presumably abbots') orchards. There was, he observed, a 'new breed' of monks who were busy rooting out the old and neglected trees and planting various fruit trees that had been brought from overseas or bought at markets and fairs.

The new brethren, in many ways less conventional than those who kept the Benedictine rule before the plague, emptied the choir stalls and the lay brothers' dormitories, and were more like the monks who had built the early monasteries and had fought off wild beasts, heathen raiders and starvation. They were not afraid to work and, from sheer necessity, disregarded the hitherto rigid division of labour between villein, servant, lay brother and choir monk.

One of these was a well-educated young monk called Francis, the son of a nobleman who was well versed in vine-growing and horticulture. He soon set about persuading other members of his community in one of the southern counties of England to revive their interest in the growing of fruit other than the grape and the apple.

He began with plums, for there was much evidence in the monastery garden that the monks of an earlier age had grown them. He had known from his reading and talk with the learned monks that wild plums would always have been available and that the cultivated variety was popular as far back as the early ninth century – indeed, the Emperor Charlemagne had included the plum in the list of fruits to be grown in his time.

On a visit to Glastonbury, Francis had read an Anglo Saxon herbal which revealed that the popular plum was often grafted with sloe as the rootstock. He therefore

The Medlar Tree

And as I stood and caste aside mine eie
I was ware of the fairest medlar tree,
That ever yet in all my life I sie.
As full of blossoms as it might be
Thereon a goldfinch leaping pretile
Fro bough to bough and as him list, he cet
Here and there of buds and floures sweet.

resolved to plant an entire orchard of plums using this method. The need for plums existed at the monastery, for one of the cooks who enjoyed experimenting with dishes of former times was buying the fruit from a local garden. He beat the plums into a pulp, which he then thickened with flour and breadcrumbs, adding sugar, spices and colouring. He served the plum mixture as a special 'murrey' to please the abbot.

Francis also began to rekindle an interest in the cherry, having heard that new varieties of the fruit had been distributed from Rome to other countries even as far as Britain by 42BC. Monk-gardeners before him would certainly have had cherry trees. The fruit was one of several praised in a poem by Neckam, the twelfth-century Abbot of Cirencester, and at Norwich the monks maintained a special garden called the cherruzerd or orto cersor. The monks of Ely were also fond of cherries and they even grew enough in 1302 to have a surplus of the fruit for sale.

Few monastery gardens would have been short of peaches for the fruit had been popular for many years and the trees, although large, had not grown wild. Some had been fan-trained along walls and flourished in the sun. Many peaches dropped to the ground before they were ripe, while others fell prey to thrushes and blackbirds, but there was always a good supply.

A tale told about this time concerned King John, who had died at Newark in the early thirteenth century after eating a large bowl of peaches. Hearing of this tragedy, an abbot refused to eat the newly discovered fruit. The choir monks, who also feared the fruit, refused to eat it likewise. The lay brothers, however, all of whom enjoyed the hitherto forbidden fruit, were able to consume the entire crop each year.

The 'peche' was described in the *Grete Herball* of 1526 as 'colde and moyste' and 'pryncypally good yf they be eate fastynge'. Oil made from peach kernels was good against 'payne of the eares'.

At another monastery, the gardener's pride of place was given to the medlars and the mulberries. The medlars, standing as sentinels along the broad carriageway from the entrance gate to the busy tradesmen's workshops, had been planted as ornamental trees and were probably a gift from a visiting dignitary.

One of the brethren was so attracted by the blossom that he spoke of it frequently. The novice master therefore set him the task of learning a poem from 'The Flower and the Leaf', dated about 1450.

Later in the year he discovered to his consternation that although clearly ripe, the flat fruit the medlars produced was left on the branches to rot. Even when they had turned a deep brown and became soft inside like an over-ripe fig, no one picked them. The monk therefore asked the cellarer why the fruit was going to waste when it could have been used to feed at least one of the many beggars at the gate.

'Bide your time,' the cellarer answered, 'and in a day or two the abbot's men will be around the trees with baskets like flies around a pudding, and in an hour there won't be a medlar fruit in sight.'

As the cellarer predicted, so the fruit was picked. The abbot, who particularly enjoyed the fruit, served them when the port was being passed at the end of a meal. The bishop, who also enjoyed the fruit and, like Chaucer in 'The Reeve's Tale', called it an 'opener' to show his knowledge of the poet, always timed his visit of inspection of the monastery to coincide with medlar time. He had discovered the fruit had been eaten for years to help with the digestion of food, which was probably the reason why it was served after meals.

The *Grete Herball* reinforces this view, for it states that medlars comfort the stomach and are more 'usefull for medycyn then for meate, for they nouryshe but lytell'. Unlike other fruit, the medlar was not 'grevous to the substance of the stomake and senewy sydes thereof'.

Medlar

The Mulberry Tree

At a religious house in the lowlands, the merit of the abbey's three mulberry trees was that they heralded the arrival of spring with a triumphant blaze of blossom that produced an abundance of fruit. Heresbachius wrote of the fruit in 1578: *'he (the mulberie) is ripe with the first, and buddeth out so hastily, as in one night with a noise he thrusteth out his leaves'*.

The large juicy fruits of the giant mulberries were used mainly to make wine, although the precentor followed the old custom each year of sending a servant to gather a

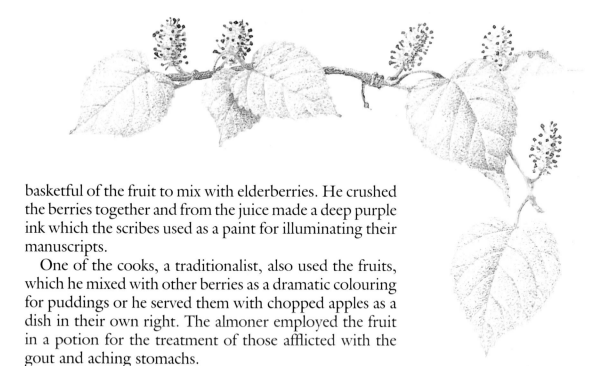

basketful of the fruit to mix with elderberries. He crushed the berries together and from the juice made a deep purple ink which the scribes used as a paint for illuminating their manuscripts.

One of the cooks, a traditionalist, also used the fruits, which he mixed with other berries as a dramatic colouring for puddings or he served them with chopped apples as a dish in their own right. The almoner employed the fruit in a potion for the treatment of those afflicted with the gout and aching stomachs.

The monk-gardener here, Brother Thomas, had a particular love of mulberries. When he learned that the mulberry leaf was the food of silk-worms and that in the orient particular trees were revered and cultivated especially for that purpose, he persuaded a fellow monk who was visiting Rome to try to purchase some saplings. The idea of producing silk to help balance the abbey's budget had wide support, but the silk-worms did not arrive and the scheme was dropped.

GRAFTING FRUIT TREES

At Glastonbury Abbey in Somerset or Melrose Abbey in Scotland visitors would compliment the monk gardener on his skill in grafting apple and pear trees. For it was a well recognized fact in medieval days that planting a pip from a particular variety of apple was no guarantee that the fruit would have the same flavour or keeping qualities. Grafting was one solution that ensured the fruit picked was the same variety as the scion. A monk was a welcome visitor at other monasteries if during the spring he arrived with a handful of scions of say, an apple with a crisp sweet taste. Perhaps too he could find time to stay and help the gardener with this skilled horticultural operation.

Technical Terms

Scion A Shoot 4–5 ins (9–12cms) long of a tree bearing several fruiting buds.

Rootstock The original tree on which the graft is to be performed. It can also be a selected rooted tree planted the previous year. Today these can be bought from specialised nurseries.

Grafting This is the union of scion and rootstock so that the two become one living unit. The tree formed will have the vigour of the rootstock and the fruiting quality of the scion.

Present day grafting

Gardeners in this century know that a favourite but aged apple tree can be given a new lease of life by grafting on scions cut from a good cropping tree such as a Bramley Seedling. It is also possible to buy rooting stock from a specialised fruit nursery and grow the tree of your choice. In this way rare varieties of fruit can be propagated, and preserved for future generations.

Whip Budding

YOU NEED:

Rootstock which has been planted in the garden for at least a year

A scion from the tree you wish to propagate

A sharp knife

Plastic tape and grafting wax (from the local garden centre)

METHOD:

Cut the root stock down to about 6in (10cm) from the ground and on the top surface cut a 'V' shaped notch. At the base of the scion cut a matching notch, then across the top of the shoot make a clean cut just above a healthy fruiting bud. Fix the base of the scion into the notch on the top surface of the rootstock and bind the join firmly together with plastic tape. Warm the wax and paint over the joins to form a seal. Whip grafting is generally done in March or April to take advantage of spring growth.

Servants of the Monastery

THE MONK-GARDENER

The monk-gardener of every Cistercian monastery in the early part of the sixteenth century would have had a companionable life with no lack of responsibilities. His influence would have been considerable and wide ranging. As the scarce but valuable records show, hardly an activity took place without some contribution from him and his assistants. His managerial abilities and the skills and products of his hired workers at the abbey and outlying granges were always in demand.

Many of the monastery officials – the obedientiaries – relied to a great extent on what the soil within the monastery wall produced. Some officials had their own gardens – or 'medes' – and either tended them as part of their work or had servants to do it for them. In most cases, the obedientiaries were keen to accept the help and advice of a professional.

The hard-pressed and hard-working cellarer would have relied on the gardener for more than just an ample harvest from the abbey's gardens, important though that was. He would have wanted advice and practical assistance too, and if, for example, the coat of the abbot's favourite horse lost its sheen prior to the bishop's visit of inspection, the cellarer would have turned to the gardener for advice for he was the expert on herbal remedies.

The gardener knew well that to please the cellarer he had to produce beans and onions, garlic and green vegetables in quantity. 'Grow enough to go round' shouted the official at one abbey as he rode across the courtyard

Plants used for dyeing:
Tansy (yellow or orange)
Cow parsley (yellow)
woad (blue)
yellow flag (yellow)
parsley (green)
dandelion (magenta)
Lady's bedstraw (orange-red)

– which was not always found in monastic gardens – and the wood of elder. Both woods were burned to heat the water which was used for the well-regulated and ceremonial shaving and washing of heads.

The gardener also supplied the herb soapwort – commonly called Bouncing Bet – from which the chamberlain's men made soap for the razor's edge. He sold a variety of antiseptic and sweet herbs from the garden to staunch the flow of blood when a razor had slipped.

The chamberlain's demands did not end there, however. He also knew of the gardener's secret plots of land and especially sown areas from which a wide range of dye-yielding plants such as madder and woad could be obtained for the tailors. He also needed teazles and flax for the cloth-makers, specially grown corn to feed the abbot's hens – and perhaps some goosefoot and a newly introduced cabbage together with a bag of young parsley for the tiny warren of rabbits that he maintained against the rule for his own benefit.

THE FRATERER

Like the chamberlain, the fraterer also sought strewing herbs. Among his onerous and time-consuming duties was to furnish the tables, seats, linen, crockery and the means of eating meals. Rushes, straw and herbs were his main requirements, but he also sought a plentiful supply of flowers, fennel, mint and other aromatic herbs for the tables and to scatter to make, as St Benedict had put it, 'a sweet odour'.

The fraterer would visit the gardener to obtain twigs of broom to make besoms for cleaning the frater floor, small brushes to clear the tables of crumbs which were then sent to the almoner, and long-handled brooms to reach the beams where spiders spun their webs. In the warm weather, the fraterer would visit the abbey gardens to obtain baskets of fresh green mint which would be rubbed into the tables to produce an appetising aroma.

THE KITCHENER

Although a busy man, a frequent caller at the monk-gardener's shed was the kitchener. His duty was to ensure a regular supply of food for all who lived and worked beneath the abbey's many roofs, and his interest in the vegetable gardens, fish-ponds and rabbit warrens was always keen. He also had a duty, laid on him by a chapter of the rule, to visit the sick and to ensure that they were fed.

On the kitchener rested the unwelcome task of keeping a sharp eye on the cooks, to make sure that the main meal of the day was ready on time and to see that one of his assistants, the larderer, was properly supplied with meat and fish, fowls and others birds.

Luxuries were obtained from the gardener by the Guest Master for his guests

THE LARDERER

The larderer, a man whom St Benedict had suggested should be 'as perfect, just, faithful a servant as could be found' was generally so, bearing in mind the temptations that were put before him. He had charge of the keys of the out-houses that were attached to the larder and he was responsible for the hay house and stores.

Like the modern butcher, the larderer had to supervise the killing and skinning of all live animals and their preparation for the spit, which meant that he was often in a strong position to bargain and to offer gifts.

The many cooks with whom the monk-gardener did business included those serving at various stations in the monastery's main kitchens and special workers such as the pittance (extra food) cook, the infirmary cook, the guest-house cooks, the fish cook and those who worked in the salting house and in the bakery.

THE GUEST-HOUSE MASTER

The guest-master also appeared frequently at the gardener's door, but, since he was an important official, he relied on one of his assistants to arrange delivery of such items as herbs to keep his many beds free from insects. When the guest-master approached the monk-gardener directly, it was to obtain succulent morsels such as sparrows' eggs (normally set aside for the abbot), asparagus (rarely found on an ordinary monk's plate), strawberries (preferably just before their due season) and only the very best of the plums, apples and pears. These luxuries were for his guests for he lived according to a quotation from a chapter of the rule which said: 'All guests who come shall be received as though they were Christ; for He Himself said, "I was a stranger and ye took Me in".'

The guest-master's duty was to show a cheerful countenance and to provide agreeable conversation, thereby increasing the reputation of the monastery, blunting animosities and multiplying friendships. He also sought sweet plants for strewing on the floors of the bed chambers and dining-rooms and a plentiful supply of aromatic wood for stoking the fires late at night when the guests were sleeping over their wine and ale.

Healing Herbs

with a wattle fence and it had a locked iron gate with a notice that warned monks and servants not to enter. This, Gerald advised all who asked, was his poisonous garden. Here he grew among scores of other herbs the opium poppy for cough syrups, deadly nightshade for gout and eye troubles, foxglove for those with trembling hearts, black root as a laxative and wormwood as a worm expeller.

The second garden was open to all members of the community but it was intended particularly for the convalescent and the elderly. Here, planted by infirmarers of earlier years, were shade-giving and useful medicinal trees such as ash, apple, pear, cherry, spindle, medlar and quince. The garden had a large grassed area where the sick and convalescent could stretch their limbs, play bowls or practise archery and other games.

With the help of Stephen and two other monks, Brother Gerald had dug a small pond which he stocked with colourful carp and water-loving plants. Around the edges of the greensward – a turfed area which he encouraged 'those not so sick that they can't handle a sickle' to keep trim – he had planted beds of mint, angelica, thyme, marjoram, soapwort, rue and many other herbs for his dispensary.

He had edged the garden with quick-thorn to provide a sense of enclosure and to try to keep out mice, rabbits, foxes and stoats. Secretly, he blamed the abbot's peacocks and the cellarer's doves and pigeons for the loss of his plants, but knew better than to sow the seeds of strife.

The atmosphere of the monastic era is recreated in this small garden using a selection of traditional herbs

BLOOD-LETTING

The infirmarer also kept chickens – normally the job of another obedientiary – because he needed fresh eggs for a variety of treatments, including the special meal offered to monks who had come to the infirmary to be bled. This practice, which was discontinued in some monasteries on the advice of private surgeons, involved removing old blood from the system to allow the body to create a fresh and healthier supply.

Herbs and gardens played no part in the ritual during the first day, but they were vital during the following three days of the treatment. Each monk was blooded in the infirmary four times a year and they arrived in groups of two to six during February, April, September and October. There was no blooding at harvest time, Advent, Lent and during the great feasts of Christmas, Easter and Pentecost.

The infirmarer took blood by making a cut in the arm. So many monks fainted that all who felt weak in the stomach before reporting to the infirmary could be fortified with food and drink. When the slyptic had been applied and the bandages fastened, the patients were given salt-washed sage and parsley from the garden and a

Blood-letting took place four times a year and the monks arrived in groups of two to six

special dish of soft eggs from free-range hens while they sat by the fire.

Although the rule of silence was maintained during meal-times, conversation was permitted at other times provided it was on medicinal and religious subjects. Those who had been blooded were permitted to walk in the second garden, to search for the nests of birds in the hedge, to practise bowls and to read, aloud if they wished, from the gospels.

The monks who had been bled were also allowed to feed Brother Gerald's rabbits. Brother Gerald had begun the tiny rabbit warren as a source of fresh meat for the infirmary, but when the time came to kill the first of the animals, he hesitated for a while and eventually was unable to kill any of the captive creatures. Instead, he sent his patients to a special room by the kitchen which had been set aside for the sick and those allowed to eat meat.

Gerald discovered that the rabbits cheered the sick and the elderly, particularly those monks for whom the vow of silence had become troublesome. Despite their feebleness, they found a peaceful occupation in foraging for rabbit food and in communicating with the gentle little creatures.

THE INFIRMARY

The infirmary and its garden was also a safe haven for members 'struck with illness so sudden that they lost the strength of their limbs in an instant' and for others 'in weak health from irksomeness of life in the cloister, the long-continued silence, fatigue in the quire, extension of fasting and sleeplessness from overwork'.

In contrast, the infirmarer was bound to find space and sympathy for monks who were suffering from 'overloading of their stomachs by drinking and sitting up late with guests, and who move about as though half dead'.

If their condition required it, patients were allowed to soak their bodies in a bath that contained healing herbs. This was rare, for bathing was regarded as a worldly indulgence that was only too easily connected with more serious lapses.

Long before St Benedict wrote his rule for the monastic way of life, St Augustine also proclaimed the same restriction regarding bathing. In the precepts for cloistered life which became the foundation of the Augustinian and Dominican rules, excessive care in washing of garments was forbidden 'lest a too great desire for cleanliness of vesture infect your soul with inward uncleanness'. St Augustine continued:

> Let permission not be refused to wash even the body . . . in baths, when sickness renders this necessary. Let this be done by advice of the doctor, and without murmur, so that, even though the Brother be unwilling, he may yet do, at his superior's bidding, that which he ought to do for his health. If however he desire to bathe, and it be perchance not to his advantage, then let not this desire be humoured.

St Benedict in his rule agreed with this advice:

> The use of baths should be allowed to the sick as often as is desirable, but to the healthy and the young this should not be granted very often.

This was interpreted as practically prohibitive of all public baths and of swimming in river, sea or lake.

Choir monks who had grown hoarse from chanting in the chill night air were frequent visitors to the infirmary. Brother Gerald would have prescribed a daily gargle of mallow, for the herb had unequalled soothing qualities and the power to reduce inflammation. Other ingredients of the decoction were freshly picked violets, lavender florets and leaves of colewort. In some abbeys, those with problems of the throat were also advised to drink a tea, or infusion, made from wild thyme, anise and agrimony.

Marigold was another of the infirmarer's favourite herbs. Like the mallow, an inveterate sun-seeker, the marigold was used to make an effective eye-bath. Gerald offered it to scribes who had laboured too fondly and for too long over their parchments and for the removal of corns, warts and – a most common complaint – chilblains.

HERBAL REMEDIES

Brother Gerald relieved acid stomachs with an infusion of lavender, mint and a pinch of dried chamomile. Anxiety was dispelled with a mixture of garlic, hawthorn, poppy, balm, sage, thyme and violet. For burns Brother Gerald made poultices of borage, milk thistle and nettle, together with a mixture of other herbs.

The infirmarer recommended garlic for bad circulation, thyme for colds, rosemary for a stiff neck, meadowsweet for diarrhoea, mullein for fits, and dandelion for 'the itch'. Lice, he argued, were best dealt with by rubbing the skin with lavender or thyme; migraine required a compress of fennel or parsley; a nose-bleed required a cloth soaked in the water of ladies mantle and for toothache he advised sufferers to chew cress.

The seeds of the sharp-scented yet fairly sweet giant hogweed, or cow parsley, were gathered as a medicinal harvest. They were considered helpful in controlling fits and other sudden movements of the body. The hogweed fruits were made into a tea to relieve swellings caused by a chill in the stomach. This also aided digestion and promoted a good appetite.

INFUSIONS AND DECOCTIONS

The infirmarer made an infusion by pouring boiling water on to the plant material and leaving it to brew for several minutes. The brewing time depended on the type of flower, leaf or root being used. He may have allowed an infusion of mint or balm to stand for five minutes before removing the herb and offering a cup to the patient as a warm drink. Roots, which would have been chopped, were infused for ten minutes or longer.

For a decoction, plants were soaked in water, which would have been cold, lukewarm or boiling depending

Cornflower

Marigold

on the required result. Decoctions were normally made from stalks, bark, stems, roots and seeds.

A maceration took longer to make. Leaves, flowers and roots were soaked in wine, cider or beer for up to fifteen days – or just half a day if water was being used. The aim was to develop cultures of bacteria.

The best juice was obtained from freshly gathered herbs which were crushed with a pestle and then strained through a fine cloth which had been specially washed and dried.

For powder making, the infirmarer employed only herbs that he had dried himself over a period of a year or more. He ground these down as finely as he was able and kept the powder of each herb in a linen bag to protect them from damp, insects, rodents and inquisitive fingers.

Lotions and frictions, which were used mainly to help circulation and skin problems, were made in the same way as infusions and decoctions.

Infusions and decoctions were also needed in the making of compresses, which were pieces of cloth soaked with an ice-cold or very hot, healing liquid. Unlike dressings, which were often tied over a wound for long periods, compresses were applied to injuries by hand for a few minutes.

An eye-wash was made from an infusion of mild herbs such as cornflower and marigold. A gargle, essential for the choir monks, was either an infusion, a decoction or a maceration, depending on the seriousness of the complaint; the gargle was normally taken as hot as the patient could tolerate without fainting.

An enema – a preparation constantly used when fruit was not included in the diet – was either an infusion or decoction method applied warm.

Although bathing was not encouraged as part of the abbey routine, it was accepted as a healing treatment for those seeking the infirmarer's care. Taking a bath would have involved a body wash with a piece of cloth and a herbal infusion. The infirmarer would have been expected to provide some patients with a foot- and hand-bath, and he would have used a warm infusion combined with a vigorous rubbing of the muscles of arm and leg to maintain good circulation.

*A medieval garden of herbs from Brunschwig's Liber de Arte Distillandi,
Strassburg, Gruninger, 1500*

The following is a list of plants that the infirmarer grew in his physic garden.

AGRIMONY

An attractive plant that grows to a height of 2ft (60cm) with spires of small yellow flowers.

Cultivation

Easy to cultivate. Has rough hairy leaves and grows wild. It is harvested when in flower from June onwards and the flower, stem and leaves can be cut and dried for medicinal uses.

Medicinal use

The herb has tonic properties and a teaspoonful in a glass of boiling water was recommended as a general tonic.

ALECOST

The plant has long, ovate, finely toothed leaves which are a soft green colour. The plant grows to a height of 3ft (90cm) with small yellow flowers.

Cultivation

A perennial which will grow in almost any condition. It needs little cultivation except a stake to support it in the summer.

Medicinal use

The leaves are harvested in the summer and dry very easily. The plant was used to flavour ale and as an aid to digestion.

ANGELICA

A sturdy plant which grows to a height of approximately 6–8ft (1.8–2.4m). It has large light green leaves with greenish-white flowers in umbel shapes.

Cultivation

Angelica will thrive in a damp shady position and will tolerate most conditions. The seeds of this biennial have a very short germinating time, but the plant will seed itself.

Medicinal use

The large papery leaves can be picked in the summer and dried for use in sweetly scented mixes. A soothing drink for colds and other bronchial disorders can be made by adding dried angelica to boiling water. It also aids digestion.

BALM

Balm has a fragrant lemon scent and will grow to about 2ft (60cm) high. It has toothed ovate leaves which are light green in colour and small cream flowers. The plant dies down completely in winter.

Cultivation

A perennial, one of the easiest of all herbs to grow, balm is easily propagated by striking cuttings, root division and sowing seed.

Medicinal use

The leaves may be dried, but are generally used fresh. Infused in boiling water, they make a soothing and relaxing drink.

BETONY

Easily recognised by the bright red-purplish flowers carried in whorls which blossom in July and August. The plant grows to a height of approximately 2ft (60cm).

Cultivation

A perennial, betony is easy to cultivate and will grow in any condition. It also grows wild.

Medicinal use

The flowering tops and leaves are picked and dried for use. This plant was known by the infirmarers of monasteries for treating those who were short of breath. An infusion of fresh leaves in boiling water would also ease nervous headaches.

BOG MYRTLE

Sometimes known as sweet gale, this plant grows to a height of 6ft (1.8m) and has greyish green large leaves. The flowers are insignificant and take the form of catkins in late spring followed by numerous small berries.

Cultivation

A wild plant, bog myrtle can be cultivated in marshy conditions and likes a shady situation.

Medicinal use

The leaves, fresh or dried, are used to flavour ale.

Balm

Betony

Angelica

Borage

Chamomile

BORAGE

A sturdy plant which grows to a height of about 3ft (90cm), borage has large ovate leaves which are greyish-green in colour. The stem is hollow and the whole plant is covered with hairs that are rough to the touch. The light blue flowers appear in clusters of five-pointed stars.

Cultivation

An annual, borage is a vigorous self-seeder and needs little gardening care. It thrives in a sunny position and well-drained soil.

Medicinal use

Borage leaves contain calcium, potassium and other mineral salts. It is a useful herb for ensuring peaceful sleep and for curing melancholic moods.

CHAMOMILE

This plant has single or double creamy-white flowers resembling daisies. The plant rarely reaches more than 6in (15cm) in height and has greyish-green leaves which grow in feathery tufts.

Cultivation

A perennial, chamomile likes a sunny situation and sandy soil. The small-rooted runners can be split to increase stock, but the herb will also grow well from soil.

Medicinal use

The flowers, used fresh or dried, are added to boiling water to make a soothing tea for peaceful nights. A chamomile tisane also relieves mild indigestion.

CORNFLOWER

A popular garden flower, cornflower grows to a height of 2ft (60cm) and has rich blue flowers that bloom throughout the summer.

Cultivation

An annual, the plant grows easily from seed and thrives in fertile garden soil in a sunny position.

Medicinal use

A decoction of the flowers, either dried or fresh, makes a useful eyewash to relieve inflammation of the eyes.

FOXGLOVE

A familiar sight in woodlands and wild gardens, foxgloves have tubular flowers which vary from a pinkish white colour to a deep purple. They grow to a height of about 5ft (1.5m).

Cultivation

A biennial, foxgloves will grow in partial shade and in any garden soil. The seed can be sown outside in May or June.

Medicinal use

Foxglove is used now to ease heart conditions, but this would not have been known as a scientific fact in monastic days. So the infirmarer who gave his patients a brew made from foxglove flowers was using instinctive rather than medicinal knowledge.

GARLIC

Being a member of the onion family, garlic grows in a similar fashion and has long green leaves and bulbous roots known as cloves. The globular flowers are pinkish-white and the whole plant has the characteristic strong pungent aroma.

Cultivation

Cloves of garlic should be planted just below soil level at a distance of 8in (20cm) apart. For good results, grow in a fairly rich but well-drained soil.

Medicinal use

The bulbs can be harvested in late summer and dried in a warm shady place. Garlic was a great favourite in monastery gardens. Enormous quantities were grown and would have cropped well in the warmer climate enjoyed in the Middle Ages. Garlic was used as an antiseptic and to prevent infectious diseases.

LAVENDER

Plants normally grow to a height of approximately 30in (80cm) on a woody stem with silvery narrow leaves and bear the traditional sweetly scented lavender flowers.

Cultivation

A perennial, the plant grows well in a light, well-drained soil with plenty of sunshine.

Medicinal use

To harvest, cut the spikes when they are in full flower and put in a paper bag, head first, to dry. The sweet scent has a soothing effect on the system and helps to cure persistent headaches.

MALLOW

Mallow would be grown for its decorative appearance in the herb garden as well as for its uses. Reaching a height of 4ft (120cm), the spiky mauve flowers bloom throughout the summer.

Cultivation

Mallow can be grown from seed or rooted cuttings and will thrive in full sun or in a partly shaded position.

Medicinal use

Dried flowers and leaves can be used in an infusion for the relief of sore throats.

MARIGOLD

A decorative flower with rows of flat orange and yellow petals around a central disc. The plant can reach a height of 2ft (60cm).

Cultivation

A very hardy annual, marigolds will grow on the poorest of soils but they prefer plenty of sunshine. Seed is best grown in the growing position for the first year. It will then seed itself.

Medicinal use

The petals, either fresh or dried, possess healing and antiseptic qualities. Mixed with goose grease, the infirmarer would have made a soothing balm for cuts, grazes and insect bites.

MARJORAM

A low-growing plant that quickly spreads to form circular clumps. It has ovate leaves and white or pink flowers which bloom from June to September, with a sweet scent.

Cultivation

Being a native of the Mediterranean, marjoram likes a warm sunny sheltered spot and a rich loamy soil. The plant tends to sprawl and needs cutting back and trimming during the summer.

Medicinal use

The leaves can be dried and used to make a tisane to ease colds. Fresh sprigs of marjoram can be gently warmed and placed on aching limbs to soothe rheumatic pains.

MINT

Light green pointed leaves with toothed edges and the fresh clean scent make this plant easily identifiable. It grows to a height of 2ft (60cm) and has pinkish-white flowers.

Cultivation

A hardy perennial, mint grows well in a semi-shaded position. Underground runners spread quickly and, if left undisturbed, mint will take over a herb garden.

Medicinal use

The fragrance of dried mint makes it a cleansing and antiseptic strewing herb. There are many other ways the infirmarer would have made use of mint as an inhalant for heavy colds and in an infusion for digestive problems.

PARSLEY

Parsley grows to about 8in (20cm) high. It has bright green feathery leaves. Greenish-white umbels of flowers appear in the second year.

Cultivation

A biennial, the plant grows well in a rich soil with plenty of moisture. With a reputation for slow germination, the seed should be sown in a warm friable soil.

Medicinal use

A popular herb in the infirmarer's garden, parsley was given as a tonic and as a remedy for rheumatic pains.

Marjoram

Mint

Parsley

Although monk-gardener to the community and well recognised as a horticultural knowledge, Stephen had never been invited to work in the sacrist's garden. This sacred place, which was termed Paradise at some abbeys, was surrounded by a high box hedge and had a wicker gate that was closed only when rabbits were likely to find their way inside. Stephen had walked around the garden on many occasions and he felt keen to work the rich soil and to cut away the dead leaves. However, although Brother Henry was rarely in the garden himself and was burdened with many responsibilities, he would not share the work of the sacrist's garden with anyone else.

'I read that garden like a Bible,' he told Stephen after mass one day in early spring when the young man had asked if he could help. 'If I allowed you in, you would turn the wrong page and then where would I be?'

'He speaks in riddles,' said the infirmarer Brother Gerald. 'But he is an old man with many cares. He has kept control of the garden too long for his assistant to show interest. One day he will have to ask for help.'

Within a few days, the sacrist requested Stephen's help and in so doing, gave him the following instruction:

'Take a hoe to the garden of flowers and as you stir the soil let the plants bring to mind the Scriptures we lucky ones will be hearing from our choir stalls tomorrow.'

'And what have cucumbers and garlic and mint got to do with the Scriptures?' Stephen asked.

'Oh, everything,' the old man answered, taking the bewildered gardener by the sleeve and leading him along the cloister to the book cupboard where all but the most precious of the abbey's manuscripts were kept. He took out a much-used copy of part of the Old Testament and placed it with great care in Stephen's hands.

'When I was a young man,' Brother Henry said, 'I began copying out those wonderful inspiring words and I am still at the task. Others sweat at their labours in the fields and among the sheep, but my work now is here in the cloister among the vestments and artefacts of the church.

'When I prepare for some great feast and deck the altar with flowers and strew the floors with herbs, I recall the stories of the Scriptures, for they are as romantic and fascinating a listing of plants as you will find among all your writings on herbs.'

The following day, Stephen entered the sacrist's garden with a wheelbarrow of tools for the first time, passing under deeply scented wild woodbine as it scrambled untidily over the gateway and scaring a family of linnets that was drinking at the water fountain in the middle of the five plots.

Determined to discover the sacrist's meaning, Stephen wandered slowly up the central path of neatly trimmed and apple-scented chamomile and studied each plant with care. When he came to a fast-spreading clump of mint, he cleared it of entangling grasses and in doing so recalled a biblical phrase from his schooldays. However, when he came to the tall evil-smelling rue plant, the herb of repentance, the following words came to his mind:

> But woe unto you, Pharisees! for ye tithe mint and rue and all manner of herbs, and pass over judgment and the love of God: these ought ye to have done, and not to leave the other undone. (Luke, 11.42)

The Jews, Stephen remembered, served mint with their meat dishes and spread it over the floors of their synagogues so that its perfume would rise up and pervade the air. Clearly, they valued it.

The strong smelling rue was a highly prized herb and it was employed mainly as a disinfectant. In ancient

SAVE THE SEED

Walking between the rows of marigolds, marjoram and poppies on a warm sunny afternoon in August or September, the monk gardener would decide that now was the time to save the seed. In medieval days some plants were actually grown so that the seed heads could be harvested and stored for next year's crops.

It was an important task and he would have sharpened his knife and cut the stems of the plants sufficiently long enough to bunch together. He would place them in a basket lined with rough linen and keep them well apart. It was important that there should be no confusion between the different varieties.

Then in the gardener's shed the seed heads were tied together and hung from rafters in bags of flax or other roughspun material. Larger seed such as broad beans and peas were laid in baskets and left on a shelf where the air could circulate to create a draught.

Drying time could vary between a week and a fortnight. It was a question of fingering the seed heads for any hint of moisture that might still be present. If all was well the seedheads were knocked against a wooden bench as a primitive form of threshing to separate valuable seed from the husks and stem. The seed was then tipped into linen bags, carefully labelled and stored in a dry dark cupboard until the following spring.

The seed saved was used in two different ways. Firstly it was needed for growing crops. Coleworts, beans and peas were just some of the vegetables in constant demand in the monastery kitchen garden. Hyssop, marjoram and pennyroyal were wanted for the infirmary garden, and the sacrist needed lily and chamomile seed for his small plot.

Secondly seed was a useful source of barter at local fairs and markets. A bag of leek, lettuce or broad bean seed would always find a ready purchaser for the monks were aware that seed collected from gardens further afield often produced better crops. It is easy to picture the good-natured haggling over prices and when the crops failed, as so often happened, the cost of a bag of seed would rise in proportion to the demand.

Rare seed brought back from Italy or France by a visiting monk or from the Far East by knights returning from a crusade would also fetch a high price for their rarity value. Seed did not, in those half forgotten days, come in the neat square packets so easily purchased in garden centres today.

Odd though it may seem in this age of technology there has been little change in the method of harvesting and drying of seed over the centuries. Amateur gardeners still take pride in saving and drying seed from their favourite garden flowers and vegetables.

Seed from old fashioned flowers such as aquilegia, with funnel shaped flowers in a variety of colours ranging from the palest pink to the brightest blue, are much sought after. A few seeds of this cottage garden flower will find a ready exchange for some seed of that popular everlasting flower helichrysum with daisy-like blooms that keep their colour when dried.

times, men flavoured honey with rue and a Greek physician had listed eighty-four ways in which the herb could be beneficial to man.

As Stephen drew his hoe evenly over the ground and his basket grew heavy with stones and grass, he saw that the sacrist's garden was a place where those who sought peace could wander and concentrate on their devotions.

He was at first surprised to find pot-herbs in so sacred a place, but then he remembered a phrase from the Old Testament that referred to bitter herbs. The sacrist had planted lettuce, endive, chicory and sorrel close together, and there were dandelions, too. These 'bitter herbs' were consumed with the sacrificial lamb at the grand feast of the Passover in Jerusalem together with the unleavened bread that was made from wheaten flour.

Nearby grew a clump of mallows, also a popular pot-herb and one on which the infirmarer Brother Gerald relied for many of his remedies.

'They represent hunger,' the sacrist said as he observed Stephen's questioning expression. 'They are a constant reminder of the plants eaten by the poor. Job spoke of those who "for want and famine cut up mallow by the bushes and juniper roots for their meat". I cheat a little, of course, for the mallow of Job was sea purslane. But no matter, it tells me something.'

Thereafter, Stephen spent every available opportunity in the sacrist's garden which he always shared with the elderly and monks who had time to pace the chamomile

to the Promised Land and in remembering them, they thought nostalgically about their homeland. The watermelon and cucumber grew freely along the banks of the Nile and, like garlic, they were the staple food of the poor. One hundred thousand men had been employed for thirty years to construct one of the Egyptian pyramids and their reward was their food – garlic, leeks and onions.

The old monk described the mandrake, which had a large brown root which was shaped like the human body. The mandrake was once credited with a multiplicity of powers for driving away evil spirits and there were many who believed that if the herb was added to a mess of pottage, it would induce fertility. The following quotation enforced this view:

> And when Rachel saw that she bare Jacob no children, Rachel envied her sister . . . and Reuben went in the days of wheat harvest, and found mandrakes in the field, and brought them until his mother Leah. Then Rachel said to Leah, Give me I pray thee, of thy son's mandrakes . . . And God remembered Rachel . . . And she conceived, and bore a son . . . And she called his name Joseph . . . (Genesis, 30:1, 14, 22, 23, 24)

The old monk also talked about the common nettle which, he said, inspired the designs of the Corinthian capitals of the early Greek buildings. King Solomon knew it as a plant of great size under which outcasts sheltered.

Brother Henry, on his visits to the garden, usually let the old monk and his companions air their opinions, but when mustard was mentioned, he interrupted them.

'Here there is flax,' he said, 'from which the swaddling clothes of the infant Jesus were made. There are thorns which crowned the Almighty's blessed head. And there is hyssop which priests used to cleanse houses of the plague. But mustard. Why, that's a story in itself. See Matthew.'

The passage that Brother Henry referred to read as follows:

> Another parable put he forth unto them, saying, The kingdom of heaven is like to a grain of mustard seed,

which a man took, and sowed in his field: Which indeed is the least of all seeds: but when it is grown, it is the greatest among herbs, and becometh a tree, so that the birds of the air come and lodge in the branches thereof. (Matthew, 13:31, 38)

The almond tree, which blossomed beautifully each spring, was a great disappointment to Brother Henry for it produced no fruit. He had planted the tree himself, bearing in mind the passage that appeared in the Book of Numbers, 17:

And the Lord spoke unto Moses, saying, Speak unto the children of Israel, and take every one of them a rod . . . write thou every man's name upon his rod. And thou shalt write Aaron's name upon the rod of Levi . . . And it came to pass, that on the morrow Moses went into the tabernacle of witness; and behold, the rod of Aaron . . . was budded, and brought forth buds, and bloomed blossoms, and yielded almonds.

Brother Henry had also planted an apple tree – 'A word fitly spoken is like apples of gold in pictures of silver.' (Proverbs 25:11) – although he knew that the biblical reference was to the apricot, which he had found difficult to grow.

Brother Henry found it necessary to curb his tongue when in conversation, for he had once known a monk who had a quotation to match each circumstance of life and rarely failed to utter it. It was an annoying habit and he had no wish to become the abbey bore, so he recited quotations to himself as he walked around his garden, leading the elderly monks to conclude that he was constantly at prayer. When a monk complained that he had too many beans in his pottage, the sacrist replied under his breath:

And it came to pass, when David was come to Mahanaim, that Shobi the son of Nahash . . . and Machir the son of Ammiel . . . brought beds, and basons, and earthen vessels, and wheat . . . and parched corn, and beans . . . for the people that were with him, to eat; for they said, The people are hungry, and weary, and thirsty, in the wilderness. (II Samuel, 17:27, 28, 29)

When Brother Henry had first taken over the garden, he had planned to remove the overgrown hedges of box which made entry difficult to the five plots which contained the plants and herbs for use in the church. The elderly monks, however, dissuaded him and they taught him how to clip the hedge into shapes as the Romans had done. In doing so, the monks referred Brother Henry to a passage that appeared in Isaiah:

> . . . I will make the wilderness a pool of water . . . I will plant in the wilderness the cedar, the shittah tree . . . I will set in the desert the fir tree, and the pine, and the box tree together. That they may see, and know, and consider, and understand together, that the hand of the Lord hath done this . . .

Brother Henry had then dug a hole to create a pool of water as the infimarer Brother Gregory had done in his garden. He endeavoured to grow bulrushes there and took cuttings of blackberry from the wild.

The sacrist sowed coriander each season, for he believed that the manna which rained down upon the Israelites was the seed of the herb that had been carried from the fields by the wind. He often trimmed the green bay tree for he used its branches to decorate the church and the infirmarer would ask for bay leaves to use in his medicines. Brother Henry also knew that the ancients regarded the tree as a symbol of wealth and wickedness and he recited to himself:

> I have seen the wicked in great power, and spreading himself like a green bay tree. (Psalm 37)

In Roman times, the bay became popular and its leaves were used as a crown to adorn the brows of great athletes and poets.

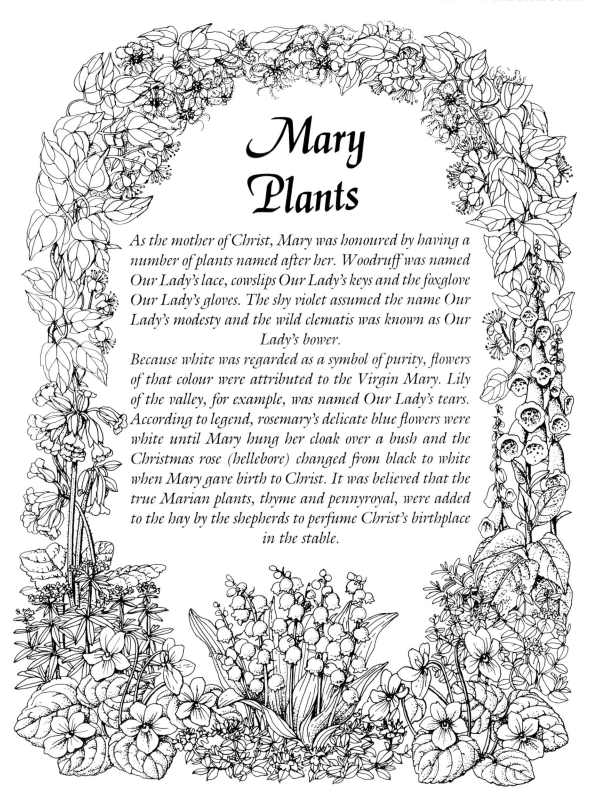

Mary Plants

As the mother of Christ, Mary was honoured by having a number of plants named after her. Woodruff was named Our Lady's lace, cowslips Our Lady's keys and the foxglove Our Lady's gloves. The shy violet assumed the name Our Lady's modesty and the wild clematis was known as Our Lady's bower.

Because white was regarded as a symbol of purity, flowers of that colour were attributed to the Virgin Mary. Lily of the valley, for example, was named Our Lady's tears. According to legend, rosemary's delicate blue flowers were white until Mary hung her cloak over a bush and the Christmas rose (hellebore) changed from black to white when Mary gave birth to Christ. It was believed that the true Marian plants, thyme and pennyroyal, were added to the hay by the shepherds to perfume Christ's birthplace in the stable.

THE MARY GARDEN

After the Reformation, attempts were made to destroy the traditional link between plants and worship. Mary plants, such as Our Lady's thimble and herb of the Madonna, for example, returned to their original names of harebell and costmary. In the early Middle Ages, however, the abbey gardeners and other obedientiaries planted and used a wide range of flowers that had religious associations. These plants were not used simply to decorate the church, important though that was, but they were displayed so that the devout could have always before them a reminder of the Saviour in whose steps they endeavoured to tread.

Provided the legends were interesting and credible, the sacrist would decorate the church on feast days and festivals with appropriate plants. *Hypericum perforatum*'s bright yellow flowers were used for the feast day of St John the Baptist – in fact, the plant received its common name St John's wort because of this. The Michaelmas daisy has for long been associated with the feast of Michaelmas.

Many saints were recognised in plant names. Chamomile, the herb of humility, became known as St Anne's flower. The tiny geranium herb robert was attributed to St Robert, founder of the order of Cistercians, who used the plant to treat victims of the plague.

Samphire was known as St Peter's herb, but he was also associated with the cowslip – a common country flower. According to legend, the saint became so angry when he found unbelievers attempting to enter heaven by the back gate that he allowed the keys to the main gate to fall from his hands. The keys took root in the cloister garth of a monastery and at once became cowslips.

Clover was associated with St Patrick who used the plant to explain the mystery of the Trinity to the Irish. Avens, which was known more commonly as herb bennet or *herba benedicta*, is St Benedict's plant, as are hemlock and valerian.

The sacrist and other monastic officials recognised that flowers offered country people a wide variety of meanings. Pansy was known as herb trinity because of its white, yellow and purple colourings. The passion flower, it was said, revealed the crown of thorns, the five wounds, the

St John's wort

Monk gardeners were able to produce an astonishing variety of fruit and vegetables

ten apostles and the spear that pierced Christ's side.

Angelica became a holy herb that was much sought after following a story regarding a community of monks who were dying from the plague. An angel told the monks to eat angelica and, as soon as they chewed a leaf, they were cured. Even today, some country people chew a seed of angelica on Sundays to keep pestilence at bay.

Trees, too, were endowed with religious significance. The crown of thorns was made from either the acacia or the holly tree and the rods that the Roman soldiers used to scourge Christ's body were made from the birch.

Pets in the Cloister

In the Middle Ages it was the custom for ladies to attend service with one or more dogs on their laps and for the men to carry a hawk on the wrist. In 1311 a decree of the Council of Vienne complained that many church ministers came into choir 'bringing hawks with them and leading hunting dogs'. Medieval writers on hawking actually advised that the fierce birds should be taken into church 'to accustom them to crowds'.

Archbishop Peckham had several times to forbid the Abbess of Romsey to keep monkeys in her own chamber and in 1387 William of Wykeham wrote of the nuns that they took with them to church such 'frivolous things' as rabbits, birds and hounds 'to the grevious peril of their souls'. He ordered that any nun found with such pets should fast on bread and water on one Saturday for each offence.

At Chatteris and Ickleton in 1345 the nuns were warned against harbouring fowls, dogs and small birds and taking them into church during divine service. Dogs were in general the most numerous among convent animals, but they were not always welcome. The prioress of Langley Priory complained that Lady Audley, who apparently rented a set of rooms within the nunnery, possessed such a 'great abundance' of dogs (twelve in all) which 'make a great uproar in the church, hindering the community in their psalmody and the nuns hereby are made terrified'.

Even such an aristocratic lady as the Prioress of St Helen's Bishopgate was ordered in the fifteenth century to remove dogs 'and content herself with one or two', and in 1520 the Prioress of Flixton was bidden to send all dogs away from the convent 'except one which she prefers'.

Dog owners took heed, it seems, but, despite many protests, Margaret Ingoldesby of Legbourne continued to 'lie at night . . . among the nuns, bringing with her birds by whose jargoning silence is broken and the rest of the nuns is disturbed'.

Despite the continued protestations of the bishops, who regarded private ownership of any property, including pets, as being against the rules, nuns singled out favourites from among the farmyard animals or even kept them in cages as their own. When one religious lady insisted on keeping a cow, the hierarchy finally relented but stipulated that if 'any one must needs have a cow, let her take care that she neither annoy nor harm any one, and that her own thoughts be not too much fixed thereon'.

There was such serious controversy over the keeping of cocks and hens in one nunnery that the archbishop himself ordered that they were to be 'nourished alike' and the eggs 'ministered equally' among the nuns. However, as the chroniclers tell, each nun retained to her own hen. Rivalry continued when eggs were counted, there was bickering over the possession of a good laying hen, and turmoil when a fowl laid in the wrong nest.

Cats were never popular with the monks and nuns although there is a grisly tale concerning the prioress of Newington who was smothered in bed by a cat. The poet Skelton wrote about Gyb, a 'vylanous false cat' who slew the pet sparrow of Joanna Scope, a boarder at Carrow Priory.

Among the exotic birds, parrots became increasingly numerous. Foreign wool merchants, anxious to please those convent officials who were charged with selling the nuns' wool harvest, brought them as gifts or 'considerations'. Not all parrots found favour, however, for one twelfth-century parrot told so many tales about the nuns that he was poisoned by them for his pains. Another, by name of Vert-Vert, was regarded by the community in which he lived as the most beautiful, amiable and devout parrot in the world. He fed with the nuns, took bon-bons from their pockets between meals, and slept in the dorter with the youngest and the prettiest.

According to the eighteenth-century writer Gresset, what excited the nuns' special interest was the parrot's ability to learn. He not only talked like a book, he could sing as well and took an important part in the chants and prayers. The fame of this remarkable bird spread far and wide and pilgrims came from all directions to the abbey parlour to hear him talk. One day, however, as the nuns gathered in the chapter house to discuss the business of the day, they heard that the nuns of a convent many miles away had sent a messenger to plead that Vert-Vert should be sent by boat to visit them.

The parrot did not travel alone. His companions consisted of a trio of ladies of loose morals, a number of dragoons and others whose unseemly jests and oaths affected the bird. According to the story, the parrot repeated all that he heard, no evil word escaping him. And by the end of the journey, he had forgotten all that he had learned in the nunnery.

When the ship eventually docked near the convent gates, Vert-Vert's cage was covered quickly against the hour when all the community and important guests in-vited for the occasion could gather together and hear the saintly bird discourse at length. When eventually the cloth was removed, Vert-Vert did not speak from the gospels, neither did he recite the psalms. Only oaths and blasphemies fell from his beak. The scandalised nuns despatched the offending bird home without delay and, it is said, his own convent received him with dismay. Nine of the most venerable sisters debated his punishment; two were for his death, two for sending him back to the jungle and five for a sentence which included placing him in the guardianship of the ugliest nun available and a total ban on his biscuits.

Eventually, however, the parrot re-formed and the rejoicing nuns cut short his penance and welcomed him back to the church and the dorter, and decked his favourite haunts with flowers and ribbons. The happiness was to be short-lived, for passing too soon from a fasting diet to one of sweets and other delicious fare brought Vert-Vert to an untimely end. The nuns' grief was probably short-lived for the tale goes that within weeks they were, to the bishop's dismay, lavishing their gifts upon a donkey.

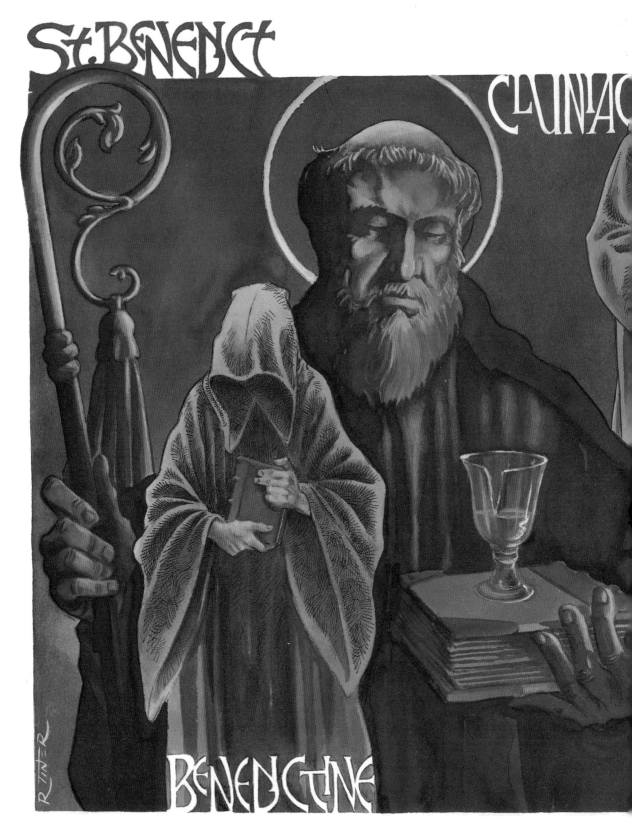

St. BENEDICT

CLUNIAC

BENEDICTINE

Various monastic orders